C000314952

THE SPEYSII

*The railway from
Craigellachie
to
Boat of Garten*

*A Speyside train waits to leave Craigellachie in very early LNER days.
The loco is Class M No.57, which was withdrawn in June 1925, while
the coaches are still in GNSR two-colour livery.*

Revised Edition

The 2.55pm Down train for Boat of Garten has just left Dailuaine Halt headed by No.62271, one of the GNSR Class V (D40). The overbridge carries the drive to Carron House while the connection to Dailuaine Distillery is a short distance behind the photographer. 25th September, 1956. (J L Stevenson)

Contents

Introduction

The Spey ranks as one of the great rivers of Scotland. Over 100 miles separate its source high in the Monadhliath and its mouth on the Moray Firth but being fast flowing and shallow it is unsuitable for navigation. Despite that it was for very many years an important transport artery as floating proved the simplest way of moving timber harvested along its banks. To-day most people will connect it with whisky and the sport provided by that king of fish, the salmon.

Over 140 years ago a writer said of its middle reaches that "nature has forced her to thread her course around the bases of mountains and often for miles together she is confined by precipitous banks on both sides, in many cases so steep that on looking at them a spectator would pronounce a railway along them impossible." And yet a railway was indeed built from Craigellachie up the river to Boat of Garten and forms the subject of this book.

Strathspey is very scenic, particularly between Grantown and Craigellachie, but the river itself is somewhat secretive so that the present day traveller on the main road between these towns sees little of it. Time was when the best way to enjoy this picturesque journey was by train. The railway was never very far from the river, indeed there were places where the track seemed almost to hang above the water. Altogether it was a truly delightful journey.

The trains were never in a hurry and while this may have pleased the visitor, for the local people it could be a different matter. Inevitably the increasing use of cars and lorries meant less traffic for the railway so that the passenger service ended in October 1965 with the line closing completely a few years later. Fortunately to-day those with time to spare can walk or cycle much of the route between Craigellachie and Nethybridge as it is incorporated in the Speyside Way.

During the years since the first edition of this book was published more information about the railway itself has come to light and, as might be expected, there have been changes affecting the old formation; all of this has been included so as to bring the story up to-date.

Dick Jackson
April 2006

An early panorama of Craigellachie. Railwaymen pose patiently for the photographer beside a class 28 of 1862 standing at the Speyside branch platform. Note the old style signals on the right controlling traffic to and from Elgin.

The Speyside Line

The railway between Craigellachie and Boat of Garten was built by the Strathspey Railway Company but this was only one of a series of companies involved in connecting the district with the outside world.

First on the scene was the Morayshire Railway authorised as early as 1846 to connect Lossiemouth and Elgin with the intention of extending to Rothes and Craigellachie (in fact the terminus would have been on the west bank of the Spey at Dandaleith and to avoid confusion the latter name will be used). The section from Lossiemouth to Elgin was opened in 1852 making this the earliest railway in northern Scotland.

The Great North of Scotland Railway also obtained its Act in 1846, and proposed to build a line from Aberdeen to Inverness via Keith and Elgin. To save money and duplication of route the Morayshire was to have running powers over it as far as Orton on the west bank of the Spey some nine miles from Elgin. From there it would build its own route up the valley to Rothes. In the event the Great North could not raise the required capital for all its project and had to be content with going only as far as Keith which was reached in October 1856.

The gap between Elgin and Keith was filled by the Inverness & Aberdeen Junction Railway (later to become part of the Highland Railway) and opened on 18th August 1858. The Morayshire trains worked to Rothes from the same date, reaching Dandaleith four months later.

All might have been well if the two companies had retained friendly relations, but this was not the case. Not only did the Morayshire engines quickly prove that they were incapable of tackling the gradients of the new line so that the Inverness company insisted on working all the trains to avoid serious delays, but there were constant squabbles about train times and payments due, to say nothing of other problems. Matters went from bad to worse, so much so that two years later the Morayshire obtained powers to build its own direct line from Elgin to Rothes via Longmorn. At the same time it started negotiations with the Great North which showed its willingness to co-operate by not only agreeing to work the railway as soon as the two systems were physically connected but also offering to subscribe to the cost of the new line which opened in January 1862.

The 15 miles between the GNSR at Keith and the Morayshire at Dandaleith were bridged by two nominally independent companies, but in reality part of the Great North. The Keith & Dufftown Railway opened on 21st February 1862 with the Strathspey Railway opening from there to Craigellachie on 1st July 1863.

On the same day the Morayshire opened its extension across the River Spey from Dandaleith to Craigellachie. The Great North and the Morayshire were now physically linked giving the former its own route to Elgin and also bringing in its undertaking to work the smaller company's traffic. It immediately realised that the Rothes to Orton line played no further useful role and abruptly closed it to through traffic, much to the annoyance of the local people. Goods traffic was worked as required until about 1880 although the track remained *in situ* before being lifted in 1908.

The Strathspey Railway

The Strathspey Railway, connecting Dufftown with Abernethy (later called Nethy Bridge) was first discussed by the Great North directors in 1860 when they instructed their Traffic and Finance Committee to inspect the country and consider its possibilities. In June the Committee reported that such a line would benefit the district and they were much impressed by the prospect of timber traffic from the large forests in the Grantown area where Lord Seafield alone owned over 41,000 acres. Following this, Alexander Gibb the Company's engineer was told to make a trial survey.

His report refers to three proposed railways, all intended to connect Inverness with Perth, which would to some extent affect a Great North line in the Spey valley. Two of them headed south from the Inverness and Aberdeen route, one from Nairn and the other from Forres. The first of these was abortive but the latter, which ran via Grantown and Kingussie, became the Inverness & Perth Junction Railway, later forming part of the Highland Railway.

The third was an extraordinary suggestion put forward by the little Morayshire Railway, which obviously had big ideas, for a "more direct route" from Elgin. This would have run through Rothes to Ballindalloch and thence via Tomintoul, Braemar, Spital of Glenshee and Blairgowrie. The directors had a survey done by their own engineer and went so far as to send details of this to railway companies "in the south". These admitted the importance of the line and felt it was decidedly preferable to the more circuitous route through Kingussie but hesitated to become involved at that time. Mr Gibb reported that it

GREAT NORTH OF SCOTLAND RAILWAY.

OPENING OF EXTENSION TO ELGIN
AND OF
STRATHSPEY SECTION.

O N and after 1st JULY, 1863, and until further notice, Trains will Arrive and Depart as under :—

STRATHSPEY SECTION.

DOWN TRAINS.

	Parl. 1 & 3	1 & 3	1 & 3	Saturdays only. 1 & 3
	A.M.	A.M.	P.M.	P.M.
KEITH, ...dep	7·30	11·0	4·5	7·40
ELGIN, ... ,,	7·40	11·15	4·15	7·50
STRATHSPEY, JN. ...... ,,	8·23	12·15	5·2	8·45
GRANTOWN, ... ,,	9·40	1·33	6·20	9·53
ABERNETHY, ... ,,	10·7	2·0	6·47	10·20

UP TRAINS.

	Parl. 1 & 3	1 & 3	1 & 3	Saturdays only. 1 & 3
	A.M.	A.M.	P.M.	P.M.
ABERNETHY, ...dep.	6·30	10·20	3·0	7·0
GRANTOWN, ... ,,	6·56	10·46	3·26	7·26
STRATHSPEY, ...arr.	8·10	11·58	4·40	8·38
ELGIN, ... ,,	9·5	12·40	5·42	9·30
KEITH, ... ,,	9·5	12·50	5·55	9·40

ORTON BRANCH.

DOWN TRAINS.

	Parl. A.M.	A.M.	
STRATHSPEY JN. ......dep.	7·0	10·45	3·40
ORTON, ...arr.	7·20	11·5	4·0

UP TRAINS.

	Parl. A.M.	A.M.	A.M.
ORTON, ...dep.	7·40	11·20	4·35
STRATHSPEY JN. ......arr.	8·0	11·43	5·0

had severe gradients with a summit tunnel of at least six miles and so he discounted it.

Not long after this comes the first reference to possible traffic from the Duke of Richmond's iron ore mines near Tomintoul. As will be seen later, this was to keep reappearing.

By October 1860 the new line was officially called the Strathspey Railway and towards the end of year the necessary Bill was laid before Parliament, receiving the Royal Assent in May 1861. The Act also allowed for the construction of a branch line from Ballifurth, 2 miles north of Abernethy, to meet the Inverness & Perth Junction Railway at Dulnain Bridge, or at an independent terminus, but this was never built.

Six months later the tender for the construction of the railway was awarded to Mr Preston of Elgin for the sum of £82,000. He may have been cheaper than his only rival, but clearly was not up to the job as less than a year later he was relieved of the work which was then undertaken by the Company itself. Money, as always, was tight and one way to keep within the Parliamentary estimate was the use of second hand rails for the last 5 miles to Abernethy. Again cheapest was not best because when the line was inspected by Colonel Yolland on behalf of the Board of Trade he refused to accept them on the grounds that it would be setting a bad precedent. The Company promised to replace the rails within two months and in the meantime to restrict the speed of trains to 10 mph, and that satisfied their Lordships.

The directors and official guests travelled along the line to Abernethy on 25th June where, on arrival, they sat down to a "sumptious lunch…..in the large new engine house." Following this the line was opened for traffic on 1st July 1863.

To-day it is almost impossible to realise the impact made by the arrival of the railway on a rural area such as Speyside. Until then most people had to walk and goods moved slowly by lumbering wagon over very indifferent roads. Suddenly journeys which had taken days could be made in a matter of hours. When on 18th June 1863 a train carrying Company officials finally went through from Dufftown to Abernethy it is small wonder that the Aberlour correspondent of the 'Elgin Courant' waxed ungrammatically lyrical. "All the world knows that a nation's history is made up of events which take place from time to time during revolving ages. In like manner all the readers of the Elgin Courant may now know that an era in the future history of Strathspey dawned on Thursday last which all the world may hear of after the present generation has gone to their last resting place".

On to Boat of Garten

Plans for the extension of the Strathspey Railway for 4¾ miles from Abernethy to Boat of Garten, where the Inverness & Perth Junction Railway's station was to be used, were considered in November 1864 but doubts were soon raised as to the wisdom of this. It was felt that the Great North's share of the traffic going south from Speyside would in future travel by the shorter route instead of via Keith and Aberdeen. When it was pointed out that the Strathspey line was an accomplished fact and that somebody else could well move in to fill the gap it was agreed to go ahead. This desire to encourage traffic to go south the long way round via Aberdeen could still be seen seventy years later — the LNER had a large notice at Boat of Garten advertising trains to the south via Aberdeen!

The Strathspey met the Highland Railway at Tullochgorum, not far south of the latter's Broomhill station, but it was not a junction in the accepted sense. As the Highland had no operational need for a signal box there it laid a second track parallel to its own for the final three miles to 'The Boat' for the exclusive use of Speyside trains. The actual junction between the two Companies was originally at the south end of the station although another connection was installed at the north end in 1907.

Early in July 1866 an engine was taken through to Boat of Garten and opening was confidently expected on the 21ˢᵗ of the month. However the BOT inspector, Captain Tyler, asked for some further work to be done on the bridge crossing the Spey and for alterations to the signalling between Abernethy and Boat of Garten. These were not serious matters and trains started running on 1ˢᵗ August. On the same day the Keith & Dufftown and Strathspey Railways were formally incorporated into the Great North of Scotland Railway.

Meantime the Inverness & Aberdeen Junction and the Inverness & Perth Junction Railways had amalgamated in June 1865 to form the Highland Railway. With the opening

GNS Class M No.59 waits its next turn of duty outside the engine shed at Boat of Garten. Its tender has just been coaled from the truck alongside and to judge from the gleam on the boiler the cleaners have been at work.

to Boat of Garten the Great North could exchange traffic with the Highland not only there but also at Elgin and Keith, a situation which was to cause endless problems and almost war-like relations for many years. Indeed it was not until the turn of the century that anything like normal co-operation existed between them. This attitude led to problems when it came to agreeing the rent to be paid by the GNSR for the use of Boat of Garten station and the track out as far as Tullochgorum. The Great North contended that it should only pay interest on the cost of the second track and a small part of the cost of the station. The Highland wanted interest on the total cost including the station work. The dispute was eventually resolved by an Arbiter appointed by the Board of Trade and resulted in the GNSR paying £854 per annum, a figure which remained unaltered at least until 1910 when the amount was no longer itemised in the accounts.

The GNSR's ownership of the Strathspey line ended on 31st December 1922. The following day the Great North became the Northern Scottish Area of the newly formed London and North Eastern Railway. Exactly twenty five years later the LNER itself was absorbed by British Railways.

Along The Line

Legally the Strathspey Railway began at Dufftown but, when completed, the first four miles, which dropped steeply down Glen Fiddich to Craigellachie, became part of the main Aberdeen-Elgin route and so do not form part of the Speyside line story.

Craigellachie station lay in the angle between the Elgin and Strathspey lines with the latter on the west side of the layout. On leaving, the railway curved sharply to the south-west to follow the right bank of the River Spey and almost immediately was on a ledge cut out of the steep bank above the water. It then ran through a short tunnel, one of only four on the whole Great North system, before moving on to easier terrain.

Aberlour lies in an amphitheatre with the river now further away from the station. It is the only place of any size served directly by the line and the local distillery would have provided much of its traffic. Before long the hillside crowds in again so that the small platform at **Dailuaine,** opened in 1933 for the benefit of the workers at this isolated distillery, is cut into the steep bank. A little further on comes the distillery's private siding.

Shortly before reaching **Carron,** the Spey was crossed on a fine cast-iron arch bridge with a span of some 150 feet which it shared with what is now a public road. Originally this provision was made for the benefit of Mr Grant of Carron but there is no evidence that he paid the extra cost of £1,500 involved! Again the hills are very close although the level ground between the station and the river was occupied by the Imperial Distillery

The next five miles to Blacksboat brought their own problems when the railway was built. The ground rises steeply from the river, which itself follows a very sinuous course, leading to some heavy earthworks. In addition, there are a number of burns to cross, often in quite deep gullies. One of these, formed by the Allt Adhair, called for a substantial three span viaduct some 50 feet above the ground. All the more remarkable since the burn is almost narrow enough to jump across.

This stretch had several interesting features including two 'bus-stop' halts created by British Railways for two more isolated distillery communities, **Imperial Cottages** and

The final up goods approaches Tunnel Brae between Aberlour and Craigellachie on 1st November 1968. The very confined space between the hillside and the Spey is clearly seen. (Courtesy Aberdeen Journals)

Aberlour was rebuilt in 1910 with a passing loop and new Up platform seen on the left. No.70, a Class G (D48), heads a Boat of Garten train sometime prior to 1923. Today only the station building and down platform survive.
(Courtesy Technical and Leisure Services, Moray Council.)

Carron bridge carried both railway and road across the Spey with the former on the upstream side, furthest away in this view.

Gilbey's Cottages. These did not even have platforms since they were served by the diesel railbuses which had retractable steps.

Knockando House was a private platform strictly reserved, at least in earlier days, for the owner of the house and his factor and "only during the pleasure of the Directors". Even in BR days it remained unadvertised.

Knockando Distillery had its own siding and not long before it was completed the owners decided that they wanted the loading bank higher than was originally agreed so as to make it easier to move barrels out of the adjoining warehouse. This brought a curt response from the GNSR's engineer who pointed out that this would create considerable difficulties in loading casks: it would be impossible to lower the doors of open wagons and van doors would also be blocked. The original height was quickly agreed to!

A few years after the line opened, the residents around Knockando petitioned for a platform to allow them to use the

Imperial Cottages, one of the four 'bus-stop' halts created by British Railways to take advantage of the folding steps on the railbuses. (K Fenwick)

trains. This was turned down by the directors who told them the remedy was "a new road to Carron station". It is clear from the correspondence about Knockando House platform that the laird of Carron was not in favour of this idea!

When in 1896 Tamdhu Distillery was opened on another piece of level ground beside the railway, it was provided with a private siding but it was another three years before the station was built. Known first as Dalbeallie (pronounced Dal-bee-alley) it finally became **Knockando** in 1905. In case passengers were confused by the lack of a footbridge between platforms, they were reminded by a sign to *'Cross The Line By The Subway Only'* - an arrangement almost unique on the Great North.

The hills now gradually become less steep and move back from the river so that **Blacksboat** is the last station set into them. For many years the river at this point could only be crossed by ferry despite offers by the railway company to subscribe towards a bridge if others would do likewise. It was not until 1911 that one was finally built.

The Spey was crossed again, this time by a lattice girder bridge with a span of 198 feet. The contract was almost awarded to the well known firm of Robert Stephenson and Sons who submitted the second lowest tender and were recommended by the Company's engineer on the grounds that nothing was known of the ability of a Mr McFarlane who made the lowest bid. This was later clarified and as a result this imposing structure still carries plaques on the ends of the girders showing the builder:

C. M^CFARLANE

ENGINEER

DUNDEE

The bridge is now a Category A Listed Building.

Ballindalloch formed the natural outlet for traffic originating in Glenlivet and, as soon as the railway opened, the Company agreed to donate £50 towards the cost of a coach to be run by George Smith between the station and Tomintoul, 12 miles away,

A nicely posed picture at Knockando before it was re-named in 1905.
(Courtesy Technical and Leisure Services, Moray Council.)

The Blacksboat ferry, illustrated in the GNSR 'Speyside' booklet.
Mike Stephen collection.

provided it ran daily for two years. Business increased further with the opening of Cragganmore Distillery a short distance away in 1869. Thirty years later the Company bought a small building beside the station which it let to a caterer as a 'temperance establishment'. This was burnt down in 1905 and promptly re-built. Strangely enough the station itself was virtually gutted by fire in the early hours of 30th May 1922.

The valley is now wider and the track ran over open country to **Advie,** a small station with an interesting history. Once again, there was no bridge over the Spey until 1869, to which the Company made a contribution of £150. The bridge was about a half mile further south than the station so when it was opened the latter was relocated close to it. At the same time, the next station, **Dalvey,** was closed although later it became another 'bus-stop' for the benefit of the local farming community. Originally there was only a mean little wooden station building at Advie, but perhaps the directors felt that Lady Seafield, who lived nearby at Tulchan Lodge and sometimes entertained royalty, deserved better, and so replaced it in 1896 by a rather more lavish structure.

Once more the hills close in and the railway is often close to the river, although by **Cromdale** the country is more open. This small station was the railhead for Balmenach Distillery whose private line, some 1½ miles long, was built in 1897. Again there was no bridge over the Spey until a foot suspension one was opened in 1881, the railway's contribution being the carriage of materials and provision of passes for the workmen. Around 40 years later the Company declined to contribute towards the cost of the road bridge.

Very soon the track was again close to the water before reaching **Gran-**

The 1881 suspension bridge at Cromdale was used until replaced by the present road bridge in the late 1920s.
(John Diffey collection)

Ballindalloch was one of the busier stations on the Speyside line. Seen here in British Railways days, it has the LNER style of footbridge made from old rails which can be compared with the GNSR original style in the photograph of Aberlour

town, much the largest town in Strathspey. Geography meant that the Great North station had to be on the opposite side of the river and about a mile from the town, a poorer situation than the rival Highland Railway station. However, the Highland line climbed out of the valley heading over bleak Dava Moor for Forres while a good deal more business was done by the townsfolk with the various communities in the Strath served by the Speyside line.

Advie station. King Edward VII used this, the 1896 station building, when visiting Tulchan lodge. Sadly it has now been demolished.

The Station, Cromdale

For most of its life Cromdale was a simple wayside station. However, this postcard view, franked 1907, shows the passing loop installed in that year. It was removed in 1921. The connecting line to Balmenach Distillery is out of sight behind the buildings.
(A A Keen collection.)

For almost the entire history of the line, railway users had to endure the confusion of the rival stations both being called Grantown. Renaming one as Grantown-on-Spey would have helped, but when this happened in 1912, *both* the Highland and the Great North adopted the longer name! British Railways finally solved the problem by calling the former GNS station Grantown-on-Spey East and re-naming the ex-Highland one Grantown-on-Spey West.

Not long after trains began running the Company looked into the possibility of building a hotel beside the station but nothing came of the idea.

From here on the country is open and, on the south side of the river at least, reasonably flat. The fourth BR 'bus-stop' was near **Ballifurth Farm,** and before long the line reached **Nethy Bridge,** the highest station on the Great North at 690 feet above sea level. Originally called Abernethy it was the terminus of the line until August 1866 and so was complete with engine shed and turntable. It also boasted the line's only public level crossing and this must have caused problems locally as a petition was sent to the directors in 1880. As a result, Mrs McIntyre, the wife of one of the permanent way staff, was appointed as crossing keeper at the wage of 1/- per week plus a house. Twenty five years later she was still there but her pay had risen to 3/6 per week

The only public level crossing on Speyside was at Nethy Bridge. The stationmaster's house can just be seen to the right of the wooden cottage.

The railway now turned through almost 90 degrees to run north-west and cross the Spey for the last time by a wooden bridge of six spans. This had been made strong enough to resist the impact of timber being floated down the river and certainly proved its strength in the great Spey flood of February 1868 when it suffered only minor damage despite almost a quarter of a mile of the embankment on the north side being destroyed. Train services were not restored until 1st May. Eighteen months later in December 1869 there was another brief stoppage when ice floes said to be up to 10" thick damaged one of the piers. Twenty years later it was replaced by a five span steel girder bridge.

At Tullochgorum, a short distance further on, the line again turned sharply to resume its generally south-west direction to run alongside the Highland's main line from Aviemore to Forres. It was the existence of two separate tracks from here to Boat of Garten which could lead to a race between southbound Great North and Highland trains, but only if the former were running late (or could the Highland be early by any chance?)! Northbound the timetable provided no such opportunities.

By now the country is open and rolling with the Cairngorms in the background - a marked contrast to much of that traversed by the train from Craigellachie. The terminus of the Speyside line at **Boat of Garten** was a Highland station and all duties were carried out by their employees. For the better part of ninety years Speyside trains had to use the east side of the station, far from the main buildings which were on the down platform, but in 1958 British Railways installed a cross-over which eliminated this awkward arrangement. Because the Speyside service followed the GNSR's normal practice and was based on the country terminus, the Company had its own engine and carriage sheds with supporting staff.

Scarcely a race perhaps, with the Great North train so far ahead as it passes the engine shed at the approach to Boat of Garten. On July 18th, 1956, either the 2.55pm from Craigellachie, again with No.62271, was running late or else the 2.05pm from Inverness headed by an ex-LMS Black 5 was early. The former was due to arrive at 4.12pm, four minutes before the latter. (J L Stevenson)

A Great North train is standing at the Speyside platform shortly before leaving for Craigellachie. The Company's carriage shed can be seen beyond the footbridge with the engine shed in the distance.

Train Services

Trains on the Speyside line were never numerous or speedy, as would be expected in a fairly sparsely inhabited rural district. Indeed the Inspecting Officer in 1863 commented that it was a "line of steep gradients and very sharp curves .... and will in consequence require to be very carefully worked and at a low rate of speed."

The first timetable, for July 1863, showed three trains each way with an extra return journey on Saturday evenings. In connection with the first Up, northbound, working a coach left Tomintoul at 4.30am for Ballindalloch returning after the arrival of the last Down train. The first train in each direction was the statutory Parliamentary which had to stop at all stations (in fact every train did so) at a fare of 1d per mile as against 1½d paid by 3rd Class passengers and 2d by those in 1st Class. To say the trains were slow is an understatement; most averaged 16½ mph while the Up Parliamentary barely achieved 11 mph.

When the extension to Boat of Garten opened on 1st August 1866 the service consisted of two 'mixed' (i.e. coaches plus goods wagons) and two passenger trains northbound and one passenger and two mixed trains southbound, the engine workings being balanced by a goods train. The mixed trains took an average of 1hr.40mins for the 33½ miles while the passenger trains required about twenty minutes less. This standard of service must have proved excessive as it was not long before there were only two mixed trains each way with a third added for the summer months only. However as traffic increased three return journeys became the standard pattern.

From July 1910 Ballindalloch was connected with Tomintoul by a GNSR motor omnibus running during the summer months only, a service which continued until October 1925.

The summer of 1914 saw the service at its best. Now only one of the three trains in each direction was mixed. The Up mail had cut the journey time to 65 minutes with the passenger workings taking five minutes longer. There were also two local trains between Craigellachie and Ballindalloch; again one was mixed.

The 1922 timetable, the last under GNSR ownership, showed that mixed trains had disappeared as had the Ballindalloch locals. Journey times were around 1 hr. 10 mins giving an overall average speed of around 28-29 miles per hour.

The LNER maintained much the same pattern of three return journeys but at various times during the

STRATHSPEY SECTION.

DOWN TRAINS.

	Parl. A.M.	A.M.	P.M.		
KEITH,.............dep.	7·20	9·50	4·5	—	
ELGIN, ... ,,	7·30	10·10	4·20	—	
CRAIGELLACHIE JUN. ,,	8·10	10·45	5·15	—	
GRANTOWN, ... ,,	9·24	11·40	·6·41	—	
BOAT OF GARTEN,.... arr.	9·45	12·7P	·7·5	—	
EDINBURGH, CAL.,.........	— ·	6·20	—	—	
Do. N.B.,........	—	7·0	—	—	
GLASGOW, ...	—	6·15	— ·	—	
LONDON (L. & N.W.).....	—	4·37A	·	—	
Do. (G. N.), ...	—	9·40	—	—	

UP TRAINS.

	A.M.	A.M.	P.M.		
LONDON(L.& N.W.)...dep.	10·0	8·40	9·15	—	
Do. (G.N.), ...	10·0	10·0A	9·15	—	
GLASGOW,.....................	9·0P	6·40	9·35A	—	
EDINBURGH, CAL.,.......	8·45	6·40	9·15	—	
Do. (N. B.), ...	6·45	6·25	9·45	—	
	Parl. A.M.	A.M.	P.M.	P.M.	
BOAT OF GARTEN JN.,...dep.	6·10	10·10	12·50	5·5	
GRANTOWN, ... ,,	6·37	10·32	1·11	5·25	
CRAIGELLACHIE,......... ,,	8·17	12·0	2·10	6·33	
ELGIN, ... ,,	7·30	11·10	—	5·45	
KEITH, ... ,,	9·0	12·45	3·0	7·15	

1866 timetable — the first to Boat of Garten.

Strathspey Section.

DOWN TRAINS.

Miles from Craigellachie.	STATIONS.	1	2	3	4	5
			a.m.		a.m.	p.m.
	Aberdeen de.	......	8 5	......	9 45	3 30
	Banff ,,	......	6 50	......	10 20	4 20
	Elgin ,,	......	9 35	......	2 20p	5 50
	Keith ,,	......	......	......	12 5	5 40
	Keith Town ,,	......	9 39	......	12 8	5 43
			a.m.		p.m.	p.m.
....	Craigellachie Jun. de.	......	10 15	......	3 10	6 35
2¼	Aberlour ,,	......	10 20	......	3 15	6 40
5¾	Carron ,,	......	10 26	......	3 21	6 46
8	Knockando ,,	......	10 31	......	3 26	6 51
10¼	Blacksboat ,,	......	10 36	......	3 31	6 57
12	Ballindalloch ¶ ,,	......	10 41	......	3 36	7 2
15¼	Advie ,,	......	10 47	......	3 42	7 9
21¼	Cromdale ,,	......	10 57	......	3 52	7 19
24	Grantown-on Spey ,,	......	11 3	......	3 58	7 25
28¾	Nethy Bridge ,,	......	11 12	......	4 7	7 35
33½	Boat of Garten ar.	......	11 20	......	4 15	7 45
....	Boat of Garten de.	......	11 25	......	4 25	......
....	Aviemore ar.	......	11 40	......	4 35	......
....	Kingussie ,,	......	12p15	......	5 3	......
....	Aberfeldy ,,	......	2 30	......	......	......
....	Dunkeld ,,	......	c	......	......	......
....	Perth ,,	......	2 40	......	7 5	......
....	Dundee ,,	......	4 2	......	8 48	......
....	Edinbro' (v.F. Bg.) ,,	......	4 56	......	9 31	......
....	Do. (v. Db. & Sg.) ,,	......	6d54	......	10 0	......
....	Glasgow (QueenSt.) ,,	......	6 49	......	10 30	......
....	Do. (Buch. St.) ,,	......	4 55	......	9b50	......
....	London (Euston) ,,	......	5 0a	......	6 55a	......
....	Do. (St. Pancras) ,,	......	......	......	8 3	......
....	Do. (K'g's Cross) ,,	......	6 0	......	7 30	......

UP TRAINS.

STATIONS.	1	2	3	4	5	6
	......	a.m.		p.m.		p.m.
London (K'g's Cr.) de.	......	10 * 0	.....	7*30	.....	10*20
Do. (St. P'cras) ,,	......	11*45	.....	......	.....	9 15
Do. (Euston) ,,	......	1*30p	.....	7*30	.....	11 0
Edinbro' (v.F. Br.) ,,	......	9*10	.....	......	.....	10a10
Do. (v.Stg.&Db.) ,,	......	9*45	.....	......	.....	9 25
Glasgow (Queen St.) ,,	......	7*30	.....	a.m.	.....	9 0
Do. (Buch. St.) ,,	......	10 * 0	.....	4b15	.....	10 0
Dundee ,,	......	10 * 0	.....	......	.....	10 45
Perth ,,	......	1§30a	.....	6 40	.....	12 0
Dunkeld ,,	......	2 § 4	.....	6 21	.....	12p30
Aberfeldy ,,	......	......	.....	......	.....	12 20
Kingussie ,,	......	4§20	.....	8 53	.....	2 48
Aviemore ,,	......	4§52	.....	9 20	.....	3 30
Boat of Garten ar.	......	5 § 2	.....	9 31	.....	3 41
		a.m.		p.m.		p.m.
Boat of Garten de.	......	8 20	.....	1 17	.....	4 55
Nethy Bridge ,,	......	8 29	.....	1 26	.....	5 4
Grantown-on-Spey ,,	......	8 38	.....	1 35	.....	5 13
Cromdale ,,	......	8 44	.....	1 41	.....	5 19
Advie ,,	......	8 55	.....	1 51	.....	5 29
Ballindalloch ¶ ,,	......	9 4	.....	2 0	.....	5 36
Blacksboat ,,	......	9 8	.....	2 5	.....	5 40
Knockando ,,	......	9 14	.....	2 12	.....	5 46
Carron ,,	......	9 20	.....	2 20	.....	5 52
Aberlour ,,	......	9 28	.....	2 29	.....	6 0
Craigellachie Jun. ar.	......	9 33	.....	2 35	.....	6 5
Keith Town ar.	......	10 37	.....	3 27	.....	6 57
Keith ,,	......	10 40	.....	......	.....	7 0
Elgin ,,	......	10 35	.....	4 52	.....	6 55
Banff ,,	......	12p41	.....	6 20	.....	8 56
Aberdeen ,,	......	12 16	.....	5 14	.....	9 0

* Saturdays excepted. b Glasgow (Central Station).
§ Mondays excepted. ¶ Ballindalloch is the Station for Tomintoul, which is 15 miles distant.
c Stops to set down Passengers from north of Blair Atholl on notice being given to the Guard at Blair Atholl.
d Waverley Station, via Stirling and Larbert.

1922 timetable - the last before the grouping.

1930s took what could be seen as a retrograde step with the re-introduction of mixed trains. Northbound the 1.02pm from Boat of Garten had goods vehicles attached as far as Knockando while southbound the 10.15am departure from Craigellachie became mixed at Ballindalloch. These workings applied Monday to Friday and ceased with the winter timetable for 1937. On Saturdays the 1.02 pm worked through to Elgin returning from there at 9.05pm. The Company's final time-table still allowed around 77 minutes for the journey.

For several years after British Railways took over little changed but by 1956 only the first departure in each direction called at all the stations —Advie, Blacksboat and Cromdale being the losers. An interesting innovation occurred in the late 1950s when it was possible

Table 223 CRAIGELLACHIE and BOAT OF GARTEN

Miles from Craigellachie	Week Days only		p.m.	p.m.	p.m.	Saturdays only p.m
	1 London (King'sC.)	dep	7UZ30	7UZ30	10U30	
	184 Glasgow (Q.St.)	"	..	..	8a41	1250
	184 Edinburgh (Wav	"	4a10	4a10	10 0	2 15
	217 Aberdeen	"	8 5	9 30	3p30	7Y15
	Craigellachie	dep	10 25	3p0	6p45	9 45
2¼	Aberlour		10 30	3 5	6 50	9 50
—	Dailuaine Halt		Aa	Aa	Aa	Aa
5¾	Carron		10 39	3 13	6 58	9 58
8¼	Knockando		10 44	3 20	7 3	10 3
10¾	Blacksboat		10 49	3 25	7 8	10 8
12¼	Ballindalloch		10 56	3 31	7 15	1013
15¼	Advie		11 3	3 38	7 22	1019
21¼	Cromdale		11 14	3 49	7 33	1029
24	Grantown-on-Spey		11 21	3 56	7 40	1035
28¾	Nethy Bridge		11 33	4 8	7 52	1044
33½	Boat of Garten	arr	11 42	4 17	8 3	1052

Miles	Week Days only		a.m.	p.m.	p.m
	Boat of Garten	dep	8 8	12 52	4 50
4¾	Nethy Bridge		8 17	1 2	4 59
9½	Grantown-on-Spey		8 26	1 11	5 8
12¼	Cromdale		8 32	1 17	5 14
18¼	Advie		8 43	1 27	5 24
21¼	Ballindalloch		8 52	1 34	5 31
23	Blacksboat		8 57	1 39	5 36
25½	Knockàndo		9 3	1 45	5 42
27¾	Carron		9 11	1 51	5 48
—	Dailuaine Halt		Aa	Aa	Aa
31¼	Aberlour		9 21	2 1	5 59
33½	Craigellachie	arr	9 28	2 7	6 4
101¼	217 Aberdeen	arr	12p21	4 47	9 0
231¼	184 Edinburgh (Wav)	"	4 25	9 15	9A38
261¾	184 Glasgow (Q.St.)	"	5 59	10 19	11A4
624¾	1 London (King's C.)	"	5 a 5	6a30	6 F 0

A a.m. Except Suns.
a a.m.
Aa Stops when required. Passengers wishing to alight must inform Guard
F p.m. Except Suns.
p p.m.
S Saturdays only
U Applies Weekdays (except Saturdays) and Sundays
Y Dep. 7 25 p.m. until 20th September incl.
Z Limited Sleeping accommodation between King's Cross and Aberdeen.

One of the last LNER timetables, October 1947

A typical Great North Speyside train headed by Class M No.57 approaches Boat of Garten on the double track section. Although taken in early LNER days the engine still carries its original number. The coaches are all 6 wheelers and consist of a full brake, a composite with centre luggage compartment and two thirds. This was the standard formation of all trains at that time.

A Boat of Garten train awaits departure from Craigellachie. The station approach road, on the right, dropped down between the Speyside and Elgin platforms.

No.62277 "Gordon Highlander" leaves Craigellachie with the 2.55pm to Boat of Garten in June 1956. Apart from the goods shed in the right foreground, the buildings had hardly altered in ninety years.

to travel in one of two coaches labelled 'Boat of Garten' on the 6.47pm departure from Aberdeen. This journey covering 101¼ miles was the longest that could be made on Great North metals without changing trains and previously it had only been possible with the Speyside Excursions. The time of 3½ hours was a whole hour longer than that taken by those trains 50 years earlier!

The introduction of railbuses on 3rd November 1959 brought the Boat of Garten to Craigellachie time down to 68 minutes. There were still three departures daily but the service was now based on Aviemore. The first train of the day made a return run to Keith while the mid-day one went forward to Elgin. All trains called at the various halts by request. Monday to Friday the last train

Passengers join a Wickham built rail-bus bound for Craigellachie at Gilbey's Cottages Halt. This was clearly before the days of providing disabled access.

of the day left Craigellachie at 4.55pm but on Saturdays it terminated at Grantown returning to Craigellachie to form the 8.55pm to Aviemore, a pattern continued until the end.

Because the Strathspey line was worked on a self-contained basis, passengers normally had to change trains when going further afield. Connections at Boat of Garten were by no means always convenient, but comparatively few would have travelled south. For the majority going the other way, the need normally to change at Craigellachie, with the consequent wait for a connection, meant uncompetitive journey times to Elgin or Dufftown, the main local shopping and business centres. The situation at both was exacerbated by the station being about half a mile from the town centre: meanwhile the buses stopped outside the shops. The 'Beeching Cuts' led to the passenger trains being withdrawn as from Monday 18th October 1965, a week later than originally intended, due to insufficient notice of closure having been given.

Until the early years of this century goods were conveyed by attaching wagons to passenger trains - mixed trains. However by 1914 the amount handled justified two goods trains daily along the whole branch with a third between Craigellachie and Ballindalloch, running through to Boat of Garten if required. After the Great War the pattern settled down to two daily trains although during the depressed years of the 1930s these were not always justified and mixed working returned at times. The 1947 timetable again showed two trains daily with a third running most days to either Knockando or Ballindalloch. By 1964 two daily trains sufficed from Mondays to Fridays with only one on Saturdays. By this time wagonload traffic was not considered desirable and since distillery work was mostly of this type, it was discouraged. No distillery could justify a weekly block train of coal or whisky. Connections at Craigellachie tended to be poor leading to long journeys.

Table 41 **AVIEMORE, BOAT OF GARTEN, GRANTOWN, CRAIGELLACHIE and ELGIN**

Miles		Week Days am TC Aviemore to Elgin (arr 5 55 am) via Forres (Tables 35 and 36)	am TC Keith Junction (dep 7 25 am) to Elgin (Table 36)	am ② TC Aviemore to Keith Junction (arr 9 28 am) (Table 36)	am	am TC Aberdeen (dep 7 5 am) to Inverness (Table 36)	pm TC Cairnie Junction dep 11 40 am) to Elgin (Table 36)	pm ②		pm TC Cairnie Junction (dep 3 27 pm) to Elgin (Table 36)	pm	pm ②		pm TC Aberdeen (dep 3 55 pm) to Elgin (Table 36)	pm ② S	pm ② S	pm S TC Cairnie Junction (dep 8 5 pm) to Elgin (Table 36)	pm	Suns. am	
—	**Aviemore** .. dep	**4 20**	..	**7 34**	**9 15**			**12 25**	..		3 8	4 50	..		**7 1**	..		8 35	8 52	..
5¼	Boat of Garten arr	4 29		7 43	9 23			12 34	..		3 18	4 59	..		7 10	..		8 43	9 2	..
	Boat of Garten dep			7 44	..			12 35	..		..	5 0	..		..	..		..	..	..
10	Nethy Bridge Halt			7 54	..			12 45	..		..	5 10	..		..	..		..	..	..
12	Ballifurth Farm Halt			zz	..			zz	..		..	zz	..		..	..		..	..	..
14½	Grantown-on-Spey (East)			8 3	..			12 54	..		..	5 19	..		..	7 45		..	..	..
17½	Cromdale			8 8	..			12 59	..		..	5 24	..		..	7 50		..	..	..
21	Dalvey Farm Halt			zz	..			zz	..		..	zz	..		..	zz		..	..	..
23½	Advie			8 17	..			1 8	..		..	5 33	..		..	7 59		..	..	..
26½	Ballindalloch			8 23	..			1 14	..		..	5 39	..		..	8 5		..	..	..
28¼	Blacksboat			8 27	..			1 18	..		..	5 43	..		..	8 9		..	..	..
30½	Knockando			8 32	..			1 23	..		..	5 48	..		..	8 14		..	..	..
30¾	Gilbey's Cottages Halt			zz	..			zz	..		..	zz	..		..	zz		..	..	..
32½	Imperial Cottages Halt			zz	..			zz	..		..	zz	..		..	zz		..	..	..
33	Carron			8 41	..			1 31	..		..	5 56	..		..	8 22		..	..	..
34	Dailuaine Halt			zz	..			zz	..		..	zz	..		..	zz		..	..	..
36½	Aberlour			8 49	..			1 39	..		..	6 4	..		..	8 30		..	..	..
38¾	Craigellachie arr		8 0	8 53	..	9 16	1227	1 43	..	4 12	..	6 8	..	6 12	..	8 34	8 52	..	..	..
	Craigellachie dep		8 3	8 54	..	9 17	1228	1 45	..	4 13	..	..	..	6 16	..	..	8 54	..	..	..
41½	Rothes		8 9	..	..	9 26	1234	1 51	..	4 19	..	..	..	6 22	..	..	9 0	..	..	..
48¼	Longmorn		8 24	..	..	9 41	1249	2 9	..	4 37	..	..	..	6 37	..	..	9 15	..	..	..
51¼	**Elgin** arr		**8 30**	..	..	**9 47**	**1255**	**2 15**	..	**4 43**	..	..	..	**6 43**	..	..	**9 21**	..	..	..

Miles		Week Days am TC Elgin to Cairnie Jn. (arr 7 29 am) (Table 36)	am TC Elgin to Aberdeen (arr 11 50 am) (Table 36)	am	am	am ② TC Keith Junction (dep 9 40 am) (Table 36) to Aviemore	pm TC Elgin to Cairnie Junction (arr 3 14 pm) (Table 36)			pm ②		pm TC Forres to Aberdeen arr 6b49 pm (Table 36)	pm TC Elgin to Keith Junction (arr 6 47 pm) (Table 36)	pm	pm	pm ② E	pm ② S	pm TC Elgin to Cairnie Junction (arr 8 23 pm) (Table 36)	pm ② S	Suns. pm	pm
—	**Elgin** dep	6 10	[illegible]	..	..	..	**1 59**	..	..	2 45	..	4 27	5 45	..	..	..	..	7 7	..	..	..
3	Longmorn	6 18	9 9	..	..	..	2 7	..	..	2 53	..	4 35	5 53	..	..	..	..	7 15	..	..	..
9¾	Rothes	6 33	9 24	..	..	..	2 22	..	..	3 8	..	4 50	6 8	..	..	..	..	7 30	..	..	..
12½	Craigellachie arr	6 39	9 30	..	..	10 14	2 28	..	..	3 14	..	4 56	6 14	..	..	..	..	7 36	..	..	..
	Craigellachie dep	6 40	9 32	..	..	10 15	2 29	..	..	3 17	..	4 57	6 15	..	..	6 45	6 45	7 37	8 55	..	..
14¾	Aberlour			..	..	10 21		..	..	3 23	..		..	..	..	6 51	6 51		9 1	..	..
17¼	Dailuaine Halt			..	..	zz		..	..	zz	..			..	..	zz	zz		zz	..	..
18¼	Carron			..	..	10 29		..	..	3 31	..			..	..	6 59	6 59		9 9	..	..
18¾	Imperial Cottages Halt			..	..	zz		..	..	zz	..			..	..	zz	zz		..	..	..
20½	Gilbey's Cottages Halt			..	..	zz		..	..	zz	..			..	..	zz	zz		..	..	..
20¾	Knockando			..	..	10 36		..	..	3 39	..			..	..	7 6	7 6		9 16	..	..
23	Blacksboat			..	..	10 41		..	..	3 44	..			..	..	7 11	7 11		..	..	..
24¾	Ballindalloch			..	..	10 46		..	..	3 49	..			..	..	7 16	7 16		9 25	..	..
27¾	Advie			..	..	10 52		..	..	3 55	..			..	..	7 22	7 22		..	..	..
30¼	Dalvey Farm Halt			..	..	zz		..	..	zz	..			..	..	zz	zz		..	..	..
33¾	Cromdale			..	..	11 2		..	..	4 5	..			..	..	7 32	7 32		..	..	..
36¾	Grantown-on-Spey (East)			..	..	11 7		..	..	4 10	..			..	..	7 37	7 36		9 44	..	..
39¼	Ballifurth Farm Halt			..	..	zz		..	..	zz	..			..	..	zz	..		..	..	..
41¼	Nethy Bridge Halt	..		..	..	11 16		..	..	4 20	..			..	..	7 46	..		9 53	..	..
46	Boat of Garten arr	..	..	..	..	11 25		..	..	4 29	..	..		..	..	7 55	..		10 2	..	..
	Boat of Garten dep	..	..	8 54	1119	11 28		..	..	4 30	..	..		5 2	6 32	7 56	..		10 3	5 5	6 27
51¼	**Aviemore** arr	..	..	9 3	**1127**	**11 35**		..	..	4 37	..	..	..	**5 10**	**6 40**	**8 3**	..		**1010**	**5 16**	**6 35**

b Arr. 2 minutes later on Saturdays
E Except Saturdays

S Saturdays only
TC Through Carriages

zz Calls to set down on notice to Guard or to take up when there are passengers on platform

② Second class only

For OTHER TRAINS between Boat of Garten and Grantown-on-Spey, see Table 35

The September 1964 passenger timetable - not long before closure.

Clearly this situation could not last and the Speyside line closed south of Aberlour as from Friday 1st November 1968. At Aberlour itself coal traffic lingered on for another three years until that too ceased from 15th November 1971. So ended 108 years of service, unspectacular though it may have been, to the local community. Once again road had conquered.

Although 'Gordon Highlander' was withdrawn from service in June 1958 for restoration to GNSR livery, it is seen here leaving Aviemore with the 12.18pm to Criagellachie on 23rd May 1960, substituting for a failed diesel railbus. (J L Stevenson)

Excursion Trains

Once the railway had been opened to Boat of Garten the possibilities of tourist traffic were recognised. Indeed the timetable for August 1866, the first for the complete line, advertised Tour No.2. Aberdeen — Dundee, Dundee — Perth, Perth — Boat of Garten via Dunkeld, Boat of Garten —Aberdeen via Keith. 35/-. The Speyside scenery meant the line was a favourite for excursion trains and one of the first ran in connection with the Aberdeen autumn holiday in 1882 leaving Aberdeen at 8.20am and after stops at suburban stations was due into Grantown "about noon". The return journey began at 4.45pm with arrival in Aberdeen at "about 8pm". For this the travellers were charged 6/- First Class and 3/- Third Class.

For some years before the outbreak of war in 1914 great efforts were made to encourage this excursion trade. Special trains to Speyside began in June 1905 usually running on Wednesdays and Saturdays. At first they were non-stop to Craigellachie but later a call at Dufftown was included. The time taken to reach Boat of Garten (101¼ miles) was two and a half hours which was very good going over a hilly road with many sharp curves and nearly half of which was single line. From the 1907 season those wanting to visit Tomintoul could use the railway owned bus from Ballindalloch. Later on arrangements were made for travellers to have a cold meal but, as the GNSR did not have restaurant cars, these had to be ordered in advance. The Company took considerable pride in the train and made great efforts to see it ran to time — and all for a return fare of 2/6. For a while during the Summer of 1908 the train worked through to Aviemore and on to Kingussie using the Great North engine and crew throughout for which the fares were 3/- and 4/- respectively. For some reason this did not prove popular and was not repeated.

A Speyside Excursion from Aberdeen passes through wooded country near Knockando. The picture is from one of the numerous glass slides that the publicity conscious GNSR produced for use at 'Lantern Lectures' in the years before the Great War.

It was not long before the Company realised that some members of the public were abusing this cheap excursion fare by travelling out to a Speyside station one Saturday and staying locally for two or three weeks. Meantime a friend in Aberdeen posted out another excursion ticket which was used for the return journey. To prevent this, tickets for the outward journey were marked with a special punch at the Aberdeen ticket barrier and when the excursion arrived back only tickets with this mark were accepted. Furthermore, no luggage was allowed.

The Speyside line played its part in the GNSR's 'Three Rivers Tour', first run in July 1907. Passengers left Aberdeen by rail for Dinnet, on the Deeside line, where they transferred to one of the Company's char-a-bancs which took them to Cockbridge at the head of Strathdon. At that time the road over the Lecht was considered unsuitable for motor vehicles so the stage on to Tomintoul was by privately owned horse drawn coach. Following an overnight stay in the village they completed the tour next day in another char-a-banc to Ballindalloch from where they returned by rail to Aberdeen.

After the Great War Speyside Excursions only ran occasionally but some were extended to give a circular tour going on via Aviemore to Perth and back via Forfar although the direction was sometimes reversed. Normally the same engines worked throughout which brought Great North locos to Perth where they had to be turned for the homeward journey. What is believed to be the last such excursion ran on the Aberdeen Spring Holiday in 1961. The train departed Aberdeen at 10am reaching Kingussie at 1.50pm where it stayed for an hour. This was followed by a three hour stop at Pitlochry which was left at 7pm with arrival back in Aberdeen at 9.41pm. "Lunch will be served and finished before arrival at Kingussie and High Tea will be served at 7pm prompt." All this for £2/4/6.(£2.22) inclusive and certainly value for money.

SATURDAY, 15th July

Keith Harvest Feeing Market; Inverurie and Keith Sales; Games at Elgin; Fast Excursion Train, Aberdeen to Strathspey and back; and Aberdeen Summer Holiday.

INVERURIE SALE.—10·22 a.m. Up Express Train is to call at Inverurie to lift Passengers for Aberdeen.

FAST EXCURSION TRAIN, ABERDEEN TO STRATHSPEY AND BACK.

Down Special Train. (Passengers.)	P.M.	Up Special and Altered Trains.	2·25 p.m. Goods Altered. P.M.	Passrs. P.M.
Aberdeen, depart . . .	1 0			
Huntly	1*48	Boat of Garten, depart .	2 25	8 0
Keith	2 *.2	Nethybridge . . .	2 40	8 9
Craigellachie . . .	2 26	Grantown, arrive .	2 55	—
Aberlour . . .	2 32			
Carron . . .	2·37	Grantown, depart .	4 b	8 18
Ballindalloch, arrive . .	2 49	Ballindalloch . . .	4 45	8 36
Ballindalloch, dep·rt . .	2·54	Aberlour . . .	5 34	8 52
Grantown . . . : :	3 12	Craigellachie . . .	5 40	9 E 3
Nethybridge . . .	3 21	Keith . . .	Stop	9*30
Boat of Garten, arrive . .	3 30	Huntly . . .	—	9*47
		Aberdeen, arrive . .	—	10 49

* Passing time. *d* Stops for crossing purposes only. E Water Engine and Collect Tickets.

If 1·0 r.m. Down Special Train is run in duplicate, second portion is to follow a block behind the first portion to Craigellachie, where it is to be taken into Main Line Platform, and tickets of passengers in Train collected and Engine watered. It will be due to leave Craigellachie at 2·52 p.m., after crossing 1·15 p.m. Up Strathspey Train cross 2·25 p.m. Up Goods Train at Grantown, and arrive Boat of Garten at 3·52 p.m.

1·0 p.m. Down Special Train precedes 1·0 p.m. Down Denburn Goods Train from Aberdeen, 10·18 a.m. Down Goods Train from Grange, and crosses 1·15 p.m. Up Train at Carron, and 2·25 p.m. Up Goods Train (delayed) at Grantown. It is to take Passengers from Aberdeen for Craigellachie, Aberlour, Ballindalloch, Grantown, Nethybridge, and Boat of Garten.

2·25 p.m. Up Goods Train (altered from Grantown) crosses 1·0 p.m. Down Special and 3·15 p.m. Down Ordinary Trains at Grantown. Work and load to be regulated to enable Train to arrive Craigellachie at booked time.

8·0 p.m. Up Special Train crosses 6·30 p.m. Down Train at Boat of Garten and 7·0 p.m. Down Goods Train (delayed) at Ballindalloch. It is to take Passengers from Boat of Garten, Nethybridge, Grantown, Ballindalloch, Aberlour, and Craigellachie to Aberdeen.

These Trains will be formed of 1 Bogie Composite, 2 Corridor Thirds, 5 Thirds, and 2 Locker Brakes.

J. LOVIE to be Guard.

The timings for a Strathspey Excursion are included in the working instructions issued for a summer Saturday in 1905. If demand was high, the train was run in two portions. Saloon carriages became available a few years later and were included in this train. Two of the tickets issued for this service are illustrated on page 61.

*Down Speyside goods train entering Craigellachie from Dufftown headed by No.62264
on 20th September 1949.*

Saturday 25th March 1967 saw what must have been the biggest train ever to run on Speyside when British Rail ran an excursion from Edinburgh back to Edinburgh via Carlisle, Aberdeen, Craigellachie and Aviemore. This had no less than 18 coaches, weighed in at over 600 tons and took 1h.25m for the journey from Craigellachie to Boat of Garten, only 17 minutes more than the rail-bus.

Excursion trains were not the only way in which the railways directly catered for holiday makers. Starting in 1933 the LNER equipped some old coaches to act as Camping Coaches, and these proved very popular. Two were located on Speyside. Cromdale was first on the scene having one from 1935-39 while Aberlour also had one in 1939 and again during the 1955 season.

The Last Trains

Most railway lines that closed had two 'last trains', one for passengers and the other for goods. Speyside was different — it had three!

The final passenger trains between Craigellachie and Aviemore ran on 16th October 1965 but on that day the usual railbus was out of action and so the 3.17pm southbound departure was formed from a single brake second hauled by English Electric Type 1 (later Class 20) loco D8028.

To allow for those taking souvenir photographs the train departed 3 minutes late but a further 3 minutes were dropped to Aberlour by one of those incidents that can only happen on a rural branch line. Two young stirks had strayed on to the railway and had to be gently edged out of the way by diesel hoots!

The conditional stop was called at Dailuaine as was that at Gilbey's Cottages, one of four which had been provided at the time the railbuses with their extending steps were introduced so there was no platform. Passengers on this train therefore had to climb down a short ladder and as three of them had very obviously been celebrating the problems can be imagined. There was the usual delay at Nethy Bridge where the second man had to open and close the level-crossing gates but even so arrival at Aviemore was one minute early.

The railbus programmed for the return north succumbed to mechanical problems and D8028 was again pressed into service, the 4.50pm departure being delayed five minutes in consequence. The conditional stops at Ballifurth and Dalvey were not called and with no traffic on offer both Advie and Blacksboat were passed non-stop thus allowing the train to be on time by Knockando. The three remaining conditional stops at Gilbey's, Imperial and Dailuaine were all called, the first two once again bringing the ladder into use. Thus the final train ran into Craigellachie one minute late at 6.09pm. The connecting trains, to Elgin and Keith, were already in the station and so for the last time all three platforms at the station were occupied simultaneously.

As related earlier, goods traffic lingered on but even so 1st November 1968 saw the end of it south of Aberlour. That day the 10.10am goods left Aviemore well loaded with 16 wagons of coal. By the time it arrived at Craigellachie several more carrying whisky and general merchandise had been added. From the following Monday the coal would have to take the long way round via Aberdeen while the whisky went by road.

The final train was a 'Speyside Excursion' which ran on Saturday 2nd November. Organised by the GNSR Association it was made up of three corridor coaches headed by Type 2 (later Class 26) No.D5313 and set off from Aberdeen Joint Station at 9.30am.

Passengers on the very last train, a special organised by the GNSR Assocation on 2nd November 1968, make the most of the opportunity to photograph at Grantown, by then officially Grantown-on-Spey (East). (Keith Fenwick)

With over 130 people on board it stopped specially at Insch to pick up eight more passengers and following a crew change at Keith had the line to itself. Dufftown saw a further four passengers join and after that it was a case of all stations to Aviemore. No doubt it was a coincidence but the train arrived at Aberlour just as the local hostelry opened for business and quite a few passengers took advantage of this!

In spite of the wintry conditions the sun did shine at times and highlighted the autumn colours, which helped to brighten up what was, after all, a somewhat sad occasion.

At Aviemore Piper Donald Brough, a member of the station staff, appeared in full Highland dress and, after entertaining the passengers, piped a farewell as the train left. The return journey was a good deal quicker than the outward one being virtually non-stop. Craigellachie was reached in gathering darkness and to avoid too early an arrival at Keith there was a prolonged stop during which "a good time was had by everybody" - the Fiddichside Inn did well! Passengers had come from all parts of Britain, a few to traverse the line for the first and last time. Some local inhabitants were also aboard making a sentimental journey. And then there was Peter McLean an old driver from the Boat celebrating his 83rd birthday.

Truly the Speyside Line was seen out in style.

O wae's me for Craigellachie
Whaur Grants stood fast of yore!
Thon station braw will silent be,
The Sodger seen no more

Change here no more for sweet Strathspey
On shining summer morns,
And here no more when cattle stray
Will diesels toot their horns!

Those golden woods by Tunnel Brae,
The river shining clear;
All nature's glorious panoply
Throughout the changing year...

These will remain, yet thou are gone,
Thou pilgrim of the sleepered way!
That we no more may journey on
When the Auld Line's away!

The Auld Line! The Auld Line!
By Carron, Advie and Dalvey!
What can replace youth's rapture fine
When the Auld Line's away!

Cuthbert Graham in the 'Press and Journal' for 2nd November 1968, the day of the very last train over the Speyside Line. "The Sodger" was the nick-name of No.62277 'Gordon Highlander'. Reproduced by kind permission of the Editor of the 'Press and Journal'.

The two coach branch train catches the evening sun as it passes the Craigellachie Hotel on its way up to Aberlour. D40 No.62275 'Sir David Stewart', (GNS Class F) carries the first British Railways livery. (Courtesy John McCann/Colour-Rail)

LNER Class K2 No.61783 'Loch Sheil' at Craigellachie in April 1956 with a goods train from Aviemore (The correct spelling was 'Shiel', but was never altered.)
(Courtesy John McCann/Colour-Rail)

Grantown-on-Spey from the south end in the early 1960s. The snow plough had been hard at work. Today, the station building still stands, empty and forlorn, with the main road running to its right.

'Balmenach' approaches the bridge under the A95 on its way from Cromdale to the distillery on 30th June 1965. The Speyside line runs across the field to the left of the engine. (Peter Tatlow)

The fine viaduct across the Spey at Ballindalloch has just been crossed by a train bound for Boat of Garten, hauled by an ex-Caledonian 0-6-0. (Courtesy ColourRail)

Cromdale station now has a new lease of life as a house. Walkers on the Speyside way, which uses the trackbed here, have a good view of the building. (Keith Fenwick)

Passengers on this Strathspey Railway train from Broomhill to Aviemore, enjoy similar spectacular views to those once seen by passengers on the Speyside line. The loco is British Railways 4MT 2-6-4 tank No.80105.

A Keith & Dufftown Railway train passing Drummuir. (G N Turnbull)

Locomotives

The Strathspey Railway was the catalyst which led to the Great North being among the first of the British railways to use what became one of the most numerous types of locomotive in the country, the 4-4-0 bogie tender engine. Until the early 1860s, apart from a few small tank engines, the traffic had been worked by 2-4-0 engines and with the impending need to work the Morayshire as well as the Strathspey Railway there was clearly a call for extra engine power. The firm of Robert Stephenson had delivered six 2-4-0s, Class 19, in 1859-61 and it was proposed to order a further nine of the same type. However it seems that Mr Cowan, the Locomotive Superintendent, had doubts about their suitability for the somewhat sinuous line now being considered. The upshot was the decision to build the new engines as 4-4-0s. These became Class 28 and from then on all the Company's tender engines were of this layout.

Shortly after 6pm on 13th September 1878 the peace of Nethy Bridge was shattered when the boiler on one of this class, No.31, exploded. At the subsequent enquiry it was shown that not only was the boiler of poor design but more than 7½ years had elapsed since it was last examined. Although the front part of the boiler was blown some 200 yards from the engine none of the passengers were hurt and of the four men on the footplate only one — an engine cleaner taking an illicit ride — was injured by a piece of flying metal which kept him off work for three weeks.

During the 1920s the LNER found that the Great North engines were becoming outclassed and more powerful ones were needed. To begin with these changes did not affect Speyside, largely because of weight restrictions on the line but sometime during the war these were relaxed and by 1951 there was at least occasional use of the Class B12 4-6-0s that had come north from the former Great Eastern Railway.

A new type of engine with a leading bogie was designed with working on Speyside in mind. Originally called Class 28 after the first in the series, they later became Class H. No.35 here was built in 1864 and ran without a cab until given a new boiler in 1882. Note the four wheel tender. The engine was withdrawn in 1920.

Following Nationalisation in 1948 little changed at first with ex-Great North engines of their Classes F and V, which the LNER had combined into Class D40, virtually monopolising the branch for some years. It was in fact the scene of the last regular working of No.62277 'Gordon Highlander' which outlived all the others and remained in traffic until withdrawn in June 1958 for preservation. Even that was not the end of its active life as it was seen back on Speyside in GNSR livery with a passenger train deputising for a failed railbus as late as 23rd May 1960!

Because the engines were provided by Keith shed other strangers among its allocation put in appearances. At various times in the mid-1950s, ex-LNER Class K2 moguls were used on both goods and passenger trains. 0-6-0s of the former Caledonian Railway and BR Standard 2-6-0s of Class 2 were used, with at least one appearance of a pair of the standard Class 4 of the same wheel arrangement on an excursion from Aberdeen. Others noted from time to time included the LMSR Class 2 4-4-0s and one example of the same Company's Class 3 2-6-2T, although that engine did not last long in the North-east before being sent back south.

In November 1958 the steam hauled passenger trains were replaced by 4-wheeled railbuses from three different makers, Bristol, Park Royal and Wickham. All three gave an uncomfortable ride and became very unreliable resulting in fairly frequent replacement by a single locomotive hauled coach, as indeed happened on the last day of passenger services. If the substitute was a steam engine there could be problems with keeping to the timetable as turn round times were rather too tight for them.

Keith closed to steam on 30th June 1960 and although diesel locomotives would have appeared before that date the remaining goods trains were now exclusively worked by English Electric Type 1 (Class 20), North British Type 2 (Class 21) or BRCW Type 2 (Class 26) diesel electric locomotives.

One of the North British Locomotive Company's Type 2 diesel-electrics (later Class 21) heads a down goods at Carron in the mid 1960s.

19th March 1952 was a wintry day and D40 No.62265 still carries a small snowplough when leaving Craigellachie with the 10.18am Down train. Both the engine and the leading carriage were built by the Great North of Scotland Railway. (J L Stevenson)

The Railwaymen

In the early days the Strathspey line stations provided employment for 18 people, nine of whom were Stationmasters, or Agents, as they were called. They received £45 per year apart from those at Grantown and Abernethy who received £50. Each station also had a clerk whose rates ranged between £20 and £30 while the pointsman at Aberlour, Grantown and Abernethy were paid 15/- per week.

Among these first appointments, "The Elgin Courant" was particularly pleased to note, was James Barron, driver of the Speyside Coach, appointed Agent at Grantown. His "selection is a judicious one for his local knowledge is complete, and a more steady and trustworthy man could not have been found". Another experienced man, J.M.Stewart, was in charge at Strathspey Junction having moved from Drummuir Station while one of the guards was a Mr McKenzie from the Strathisla Railway.

Forty years later the traffic staff had increased to 35. By then the Stationmasters' salaries ranged from £60 at Blacksboat, Advie and Nethy Bridge to £82 at Ballindalloch, the highest amount paid to any stationmaster on the GNSR branch lines. By then only Advie did not have a clerk but their pay varied widely. At Blacksboat, where no doubt a youth was employed, it was £15 but the senior clerk at Aberlour received £60. Signalmen were paid £47 to £52 with porters getting £44 to £47. Each station had a cleaner who normally received 1/- per week. The Locomotive Department employed 3 drivers and firemen with an extra crew for 13 weeks. Drivers were paid 5/8 to 6/6 per day and firemen 3/10. The

Photographs of railway staff were very popular at one time. This one, which was taken at Ballindalloch about 1923, includes not only the station staff but also the crew of the goods train standing alongside.

two full time engine cleaners at Boat of Garten received 2/8 to 2/10 per day and again an extra man was employed for 13 weeks.

It is well known that working hours in the 19th century were long and arduous and this is borne out in the Board of Trade report on a fairly minor derailment that occurred to the 4pm Up mixed train in May 1888. The driver and fireman had booked on duty at Boat of Garten at 4.10am and were due to finish their day's work at 9.30pm "or a little sooner". The next day their hours would be 9.10am until 6pm. The Inspecting Officer was scathing. "The evidence in this case discloses the fact that the hours of work of some of the servants of the Great North of Scotland Company upon the Speyside section are far too long. The driver and fireman work for 17hrs. 20mins on one day and 8hrs. 50mins on the next, and the guard for 15 hours on one day and 6 hours on the next. Even the average of two days in the case of the driver and fireman is too high, but it is positively dangerous for such men to work over 17 hours on any one day, and under no circumstances should they be allowed to do so no matter what may be their hours on the following day." The directors heeded the warning and instructed Mr Manson, the Locomotive Superintendent, to look into the hours of duty of his men, especially those referred to in the Report.

Great North of Scotland Railway.

LUGGAGE.

Ballindalloch

From Aberdeen.

Whisky

Speyside is almost synonymous with whisky, but did whisky bring the railway or was it vice versa? In truth there was probably a little bit of both. Licensing of distilleries began in 1824 and so far as those in a position to use the Speyside line are concerned, among the first to be granted were Balmenach, Cardhu and The Glenlivet (all 1824), Aberlour (1826), followed by Glenfarclas (1836) and Dailuaine (1852). Once the railway had arrived other distilleries were built close to it. Cragganmore, opened in 1869, was the first followed by Tamdhu (1896), Imperial in 1897, with Knockando the following year.

Imperial, Knockando and Tamdhu had private sidings but Dailuaine and Balmenach were too far from the railway to be served in this way and built their own lines while Cardhu and Cragganmore used public sidings.

In the Spring of 1885 Messrs McKenzie were considering a railway from their Dailuaine distillery, which lay about ¾ miles off the line, to join it about ½ mile east of Carron. For some reason this scheme, although agreed by the Great North, went into abeyance but was revived in 1893. Even then nothing further happened and it was not until 1905 that agreement was finally reached and the siding and associated connection were laid in.

Further south, at Cromdale, the owners of Balmenach Distillery, Messrs John McGregor & Sons, also felt improved communication was required over the intervening 1½ miles to the station. Their line was opened in 1897 but whereas at Dailuaine the connection was direct with the running line, at Cromdale it was made via a siding in the station yard.

Messrs McGregor bought their engine from Aveling Porter and being based on the maker's well known traction engines it had a flywheel. It was not long before the owners

Although taken at Glenlossie Distrillery near Elgin, this engine was very similar to the first one at Balmenach. Its successor was similar to 'Dailuaine'.

'Dailuaine' shunting at its home distillery. The sherry 'butts, in the open wagon, are used for maturing whisky. Each holds about 110 gallons.

decided to make fuller use of their new acquisition and employ it to drive the distillery machinery even though an extra siding was needed to allow this. The engine survived until 1936 when it was replaced by a standard 0-4-0 saddle tank engine from Andrew Barclay, a well known firm of locomotive builders in Kilmarnock.

Dailuaine also had its own 'pug', again a Barclay 0-4-0 tank, which came second-hand in 1906 and lasted until 1939. Its replacement, this time bought new, was yet another standard Barclay similar to that at Balmenach. To begin with the Great North worked the traffic between the exchange siding and Carron but in 1913 the Dailuaine engine joined that select band of industrial locos authorised to work on main lines. It not only took over the transfer work but was also able to shunt Imperial Distillery which adjoined Carron station and had been bought by the owners of Dailuaine. At a later date it was allowed to work for a short distance in the Aberlour direction when the Dailuaine filter beds needed attention although in this case it had to be accompanied by the Carron stationmaster in person.

Both these engines continued at work until the railway closed towards the end of 1968 and both survive but are not in working order. The Dailuaine engine is on static display at Aberfeldy Distillery, while the Balmenach pug is at Boat of Garten awaiting restoration.

Although it did not have its own siding at Ballindalloch, Cragganmore made history in 1887 when it despatched the first block train load of whisky. This went to Dundee, at that time an important centre for blending.

The distilleries not only provided outward traffic by the despatch of whisky and draff, for use as cattle food, but there were also considerable inward loads. Dailuaine, for example, is recorded as having been responsible for a combined total of no less than 10,665 tons in 1904 — and that without any rail connection. During February 1909 the siding at Knockando Distillery handled 317 tons. Draff was sent to Cove, Cults, Kittybrewster and

Inverness — 96 tons in all. Whisky (sadly the quantity is not recorded!) went to Edinburgh and Glasgow with the barrels returning empty. Several stations on the line to Inverness delivered 128 tons of barley with 87 tons of coal and 10½ tons of coke also arriving to say nothing of various other small items. Finally, the Great North's costing exercise for 1902/3 shows over 65,000 tons of goods and minerals forwarded from Speyside stations, the bulk of which must have come from this source.

There is evidence that road transport was beginning to make inroads on the traffic by the mid-1920s. Loss of inter-distillery movement of stocks is noted as is the short-haul to the harbour at Buckie for loading on to ships belonging to Coast Lines.

LNER records for 1938 show that the five stations serving the distilleries received 2,300 tons of mineral traffic, 18,100 tons of higher rated merchandise and 17,000 tons of coal. Outward business amounted to 5,600 tons of minerals and 8,400 tons of merchandise which of course included whisky. In other words these stations between them accounted for about 87% of the traffic handled on the branch during that year.

Despite the gradual loss of traffic to road, whisky played a very large part in the life of the Speyside line but the railway staff were only human and many stories have been told. Some of the best were related by Maurice Shand who undertook relief work at several stations on Speyside before finishing his railway career as stationmaster at Glasgow Central. "I was asked to examine a load of whisky wagons to detect broaching, i.e. tampering of the casks. They were most ingenious fellows — some of the porters at the distillery stations. They broached the whisky casks and then covered up the penetration of the cask with a material which made it well nigh impossible to distinguish that it had been interfered with. Witness the notorious case where whisky leaking was carried out in a goods shed under the very nose of a detective from the Police Department. The stationmaster was demoted to a smaller station, as was his successor."

However it would be maligning the Speyside staff to imagine that such nefarious work was peculiar to some of them — far from it. At one period thieves apparently became so skilful at boring into barrels through the floors of wagons sitting in sid-

Loading a 54 gallon hogshead at Knockando Distillery siding in the 1960s. Courtesy Aberdeen Journals.

ings en-route to Aberdeen that whisky trains were run non-stop directly into the secure Caledonian Railway yard at Guild Street.

Finally, was there not the occasion in Edinburgh where the fireman of an engine standing alongside a distillery was found to have a bucketful of the precious liquid on the footplate! Without any doubt other such stories could be told from different parts of the country.

Timber

One of the incentives to build the railway was the existence of large areas of forest in the district. As early as October 1865 one of the directors met Mr Grant of Rothiemurchus regarding the transport of timber from Aviemore to Aberdeen for which a rate not exceeding 1d per ton per mile was quoted. Two years later a siding was authorised at Pollowick, about 1½ miles north of Cromdale, for use in moving timber from Lord Seafield's estate, almost all of which was going to Glasgow via Aberdeen.

The full impact of this resource on the railway did not become apparent until the Great War when the Canadian Forestry Corps set up a number of sawmills on Speyside to exploit it. Virtually all of the timber produced would have gone out by rail but although there seems to be no surviving record of the amounts involved they were certainly enough to justify the Great North laying down a siding near Knockando with two more at Nethy Bridge especially to handle it. Much obviously came in by road but at least one of the two at Nethy Bridge had a narrow gauge railway connecting it with the surrounding woods.

The Knockando siding was lifted in 1920 but was promptly re-laid for use by Messrs Syme of Inverness. During the same year another siding was provided about 600 yards north of Ballindalloch for use by Messrs Black from Brechin who also loaded considerable quantities at Blacksboat.

Among the various classes of engines brought in during British Railways days was this ex-Caledonian Railway 0-6-0 No.57634 seen in the more open country near Advie with a Down goods on June 22nd, 1957. (J L Stevenson)

Carron station in the summer of 1958 is still lit with oil lamps. The black column on the right with the box on top is part of the automatic token exchange apparatus.

Signalling

For the first thirty years or so the Speyside line was worked in accordance with the Company's Rules which allowed only one train on each section of the single line. As was the case on the rest of its system, train movements were controlled by telegraph communication between the stations. When the line was extended to Boat of Garten the Inspecting Officer recommended that additional instruments be provided between these two stations but apparently this was never done.

Although in 1863 the Inspecting Officer noted only one passing place, at Speyside Junction (later Craigellachie), another must have been installed at Ballindalloch either then or not long afterwards as the 1866 timetable shows trains crossing there.

A loop was provided at Carron in 1884 but little else changed until the Company was forced to bring its working into line with the requirements of the Regulation of Railways Act, 1889. This called for signals and points to be interlocked so that they worked in conjunction with each other, also for each driver on a single line to be in possession of a token giving his train the sole right to occupy the line between signal boxes. Because the Great North had to resignal nearly all its lines, implementation of this Act took some time.

Interlocking and new signals were provided at Ballindalloch in 1892. Other major changes followed in 1894 starting in January with a loop at Grantown. Later in that year token working was introduced with block stations at Carron, Ballindalloch and Grantown. The sidings at intermediate stations were released by the token for the respective section. A further loop and block post was provided at Dalbeallie (Knockando) in 1899. Following the increase in traffic consigned south through Boat of Garten, loops were provided at Cromdale in 1907 and Aberlour three years later, both becoming block stations.

On most railways the single line token was exchanged between signalman and engine crew by hand, with obvious dangers when done on the move. In the late 1880s the Great North's Locomotive Superintendent, Mr Manson, developed an apparatus by which this could be done safely by non-stopping trains and all the Speyside signal boxes, except those at Ballindalloch and Cromdale, were provided with it about twenty years later.

Apart from Cromdale signal box, which closed in 1921 when the loop was removed, the other boxes were operational until all traffic ceased south of Aberlour on 4th November 1968. Even then they remained nominally open until 15th December to allow the signalmen to work out their notice.

Finally, mention should be made of the signalling at Boat of Garten so far as it affected Speyside trains. The actual junction between the two companies was originally only at the south end of the station. Another connection was installed at the north end in 1907. But even so, trains to and from Craigellachie could only use the eastern platform face furthest from the main buildings. This continued until another cross-over was provided when the signalling was renewed in 1958.

Under this scheme the double track to Tullochgorum could have disappeared as there was a serious proposal to make a fully signalled junction there complete with signal box.

Railways That Might Have Been

Early Optimists

The railway might have come earlier to at least part of Strathspey if any of the three grandiose schemes for railways connecting Inverness with Perth promoted in 1845 during the Railway Mania had been built.

The **Direct Northern Railway** would have connected the Scottish Midland Junction Railway, later part of the Caledonian Railway, at Coupar Angus, between Perth and Forfar, with Elgin, thence via the proposed line from there to Inverness. It would have required a mile long tunnel under the boundary between Perthshire and Aberdeenshire and a branch would have run from Tomintoul via Mortlach (Dufftown) to Keith.

The **Perth & Northern Counties Railway** was also based on Coupar Angus but its route was to be via Blairgowrie, Braemar and Inchrory, then along the valleys of the Avon, the Livet and down Glenrinnes to Dufftown where it would split. One line would go to Keith and the other connect with the Morayshire Railway at Rothes and so on to Elgin.

Finally the **Great Northern Central Railway** proposed to run from Perth via Dunkeld, Braemar, Tomintoul, Ballindalloch, Craigellachie and Rothes to Elgin.

On a more local basis the **Banffshire Railway** was promoted to link Dufftown with Portgordon on the Moray Firth. This line, which would have gone via Keith and Fochabers, was intended to provide an outlet not only for agricultural produce but also the output of the ironstone mines in the area.

None of these proposals progressed any further but the lure of the iron ore lingered on for at least a further 80 years. As already related the Morayshire Railway a few years later had its own ideas for a route south.

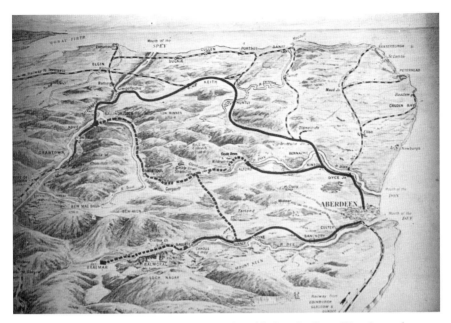

This map is based on a GNSR glass slide produced before the Great War. As can be seen, many of the proposed lines would have crossed dificult and unpopulated country.

Highland Rivalry

Moving on to the early 1880s two railways were promoted, both affecting Nethy Bridge but unlikely to have had much of an impact on the Speyside line itself. To understand this it is necessary to give some background to the antagonism and marked lack of co-operation between the Great North and Highland Railways.

The two Companies met at Elgin, Keith and Boat of Garten and while comparatively little traffic would be exchanged at the latter, Keith and Elgin were a different matter. Traditionally exchange had been done at Keith and had been included in an 1865 Act of Parliament. It meant, of course, that the Highland had the greater share of income. However in 1880 the GNSR had a new general manager who was determined to get a bigger share for his Company. The Highland naturally opposed any change and the Great North sought ways of overcoming the situation.

The Highland had a monopoly of all traffic to and from Inverness which obviously it was keen to retain and consequently the directors were very disturbed when a new route from Glasgow, which would approach Inverness via the Great Glen, was proposed. In return for the Great North's undertaking not to support this, the Highland agreed that some of the traffic between Aberdeen and Inverness would in future be exchanged at Elgin and went on to propose its new direct route between Aviemore and Inverness via Carrbridge thus avoiding the detour taken by the existing main line via Boat of Garten and Forres.

When the Great North directors considered this they decided that as it would not provide any interchange facilities with the Speyside line the latter should be extended from Boat of Garten to Carrbridge with the railway north of there being a joint venture. Needless to say the Highland rejected the idea which led the Great North to undertake a survey of their own route from Nethy Bridge to Inverness. This promptly made the Highland rescind the recent exchange agreement.

On the face of it the Great North directors were apparently willing to spend a large sum of money connecting one of their rural branches with Inverness. However at the same time a group of North-east lairds put forward their own proposal for the **Strathspey, Strathdon & Deeside Junction Railway** connecting Cambus O'May, on Deeside, with Nethy Bridge. This 40 mile line going via Boultenstone and Allargue would pass through virtually uninhabited countryside but would ostensibly tap traffic from granite quarries as well as iron ore deposits known to exist in the area. It would have had a summit level of about 1,500 feet, four tunnels and stiff gradients such as the 4 miles at 1 in 50 to 55 facing eastbound trains leaving the Spey valley. Combined, these two proposals apparently offered an alternative route from Aberdeen to Inverness but when their respective Bills came before Parliament in 1884, members had little difficulty in rejecting both.

The main benefit of all this to the Great North was to expose how unfairly the Highland treated the Inverness to Aberdeen traffic, so much so that when the latter's Bill for the direct line north from Aviemore was published it contained a clause allowing traffic to be exchanged at both Keith and Elgin.

Many years later correspondence between William Ferguson the Great North chairman and his general manager William Moffat came to light which revealed a much deeper reason behind the Carrbridge proposal. It would have formed the final link in their dream of a railway connecting Dundee with Inverness entirely under GNSR ownership. This would have run from Dundee to Boat of Garten via Ballater and then on through Carrbridge. Strangely enough, following a private conversation between Ferguson and his opposite number John Walker on the North British Railway, the latter apparently gave serious consideration to the proposal.

The Lure of Iron Ore

Deposits of iron ore around the Lecht had long excited the interest of local people and this was indeed noted when prospects for the Speyside Railway were originally considered. High hopes were raised by an analysis done in Glasgow but in the end it was found that it could not compete on Teeside with Spanish ore but even so the prospect of exploitation remained in peoples' minds.

The mid-1890s saw a serious attempt to add the Tomintoul district to the rail network. Much livestock was reared on the uplands and had to be driven to market. Similarly The Glenlivet Distillery was faced with the cost of double handling much of its raw materials to say nothing of the whisky itself— and still there were hopes of working that iron ore.

There were two obvious routes for the line. One started at Dufftown and went via Glen Rinnes. Needless to say the inhabitants of Dufftown were greatly in favour as they could see it enhancing the town's role as a market centre. The other possibility followed the valley of the Avon from Ballindalloch — a route preferred by the townsfolk of Grantown who feared they would otherwise lose much of the trade they currently did with the area. Having calculated that they would lose some £800 a year if the traffic was diverted to Dufftown, the Great North directors preferred the Ballindalloch proposal which would be both shorter and more easily graded.

Much of the land for the first option passed through the Duke of Richmond's estates and negotiations with his representatives proceeded on the basis that as the railway was estimated to run at a loss, the owners and tenants might be asked to make this up. The Duke however preferred to sell the land at favourable terms rather than be involved in unpredictable losses. The Ballindalloch route would be largely on land belonging to Sir George Macpherson Grant, a director of the Highland Railway, who reckoned that, for various reasons, he and his tenants would gain little from it. He was therefore not prepared to subscribe to the capital costs nor to donate the land but equally he would not raise outright opposition.

Locally feelings ran high but whatever the rights and wrongs of it all nothing happened for the usual reason of lack of willingness by the inhabitants to support their desires with hard cash.

Even so, the GNSR did not entirely give up and sent further samples of the ore for analysis in 1909 and again two years later, only to have the poor quality confirmed once more.

Astonishing as it may seem, no less an organisation than the London and North Eastern Railway, as successor to the Great North, found itself embroiled when it was approached by a speculator called Macdonald suggesting that a railway was all that was

Trains stopped at Dailuaine Halt, built by the LNER in 1933, to serve an isolated distillery community. The complete lack of any shelter or illumination is in stark contrast to what would be allowed today. The platform, complete with name board, still exists.

required to produce riches for both parties. Plans were developed and further samples tested but with much the same result as before. Not only so, but Mr Macdonald became very elusive. The file was eventually closed on 9th June 1928.

To-day the observant traveller on the road between Tomintoul and the Lecht will see, on the left hand side just before the steep part of the climb begins at the Well of Lecht, a ruined stone building about half a mile up Coire Buidhe — all that remains of brave proposals to mine iron ore in this remote area.

What is Left?

The rails were eventually lifted during 1969 but in due time this had a happy outcome for walkers. On 3rd July 1981 the Speyside Way was opened, an integral part using the trackbed between Craigellachie and Nethy Bridge, although there are sections between Ballindalloch and Cromdale and between Cromdale and Grantown which are not used. These 28¾ miles provide a truly delightful path through trees and fields, alongside the river and passing three of the distilleries which did so much to give life to the old railway. Whether taking a short stroll or a serious long distance walk, there is something for everyone to enjoy.

In some places it is as if the railway had never been. At Craigellachie, for instance, it is hard to visualise the comparative complexity of the junction. All the buildings have been demolished. The Elgin platforms have gone but part of the Speyside platform remains, covered in trees in what is now a picnic area with associated car park. The base of the signal box forms a viewing platform looking out over the River Fiddich and the site of the turntable can still be distinguished.

Aberlour station is owned by Moray District Council. It still has the drinking fountain body and a Great North lamp arm unusually affixed on the corner of the building at an angle. The building has been extended using modern materials but impressively in archi-tectural sympathy with the original style to accommodate an interesting Visitor Display Centre for the The Speyside Way and its Ranger Service and although this extends into the original building, there is still the tea room which is open from May to September. The yard and goods shed have in recent years given way to a modern housing develop-ment known as 'The Sidings'.

The bridge over the Spey near Carron remains, still carrying a single track road; no attempt has been made to use the adjacent trackbed. At Carron, the site was purchased by Imperial Distillery and landscaped. The distillery is now closed. The station building, which still stands unused, and the yard have been sold.

For a number of years Knockando, re-named Tamdhu (memories of the original siding of 1897), was the visitor centre for the adjoining distillery of that name. Sadly this is no longer the case and the building is standing empty.

At Blacksboat, the station has been sold for conversion to a private house while the goods shed, one of the last remaining GNSR examples, is used as a base for the Speyside Way. Both buildings are Category B listed.

Ballindalloch was once one of the busier stations and here the main building is now a hostel. The goods shed is long gone although the very fine granary has been externally restored. The goods area is now occupied by private houses.

The two small halts, Dailuaine and Knockando House, the former carrying its nameboard, survive but needless to say the 'bus-stops', never very obvious, have disappeared.

The building at Advie has been demolished and Cromdale station is now in private ownership, converted into a cosy modern cottage with external appearance close to the GNSR style. Many of the fittings have been recreated from original drawings, and behind the platform is a wooden carriage body built at Inverurie works in 1916 which is being restored externally to the original style. Although the station yard is now a small settlement of modern houses, it is still possible to trace the route of the distillery branch. Balmenach distillery reopened a few years ago and is owned by the Inver House Distillers Group.

Grantown has fallen into disrepair and there are no known plans for it, while Nethybridge is now a hostel. The piers of the viaduct across the Spey near Tullochgorum still stand but all trace of the Great North's installations at Boat of Garten has vanished.

Those who knew the Strathspey line when it was a working railway will have their memories. The rest can use their imagination — *"Did I hear a train?"*

Boat of Garten and Dufftown

In complete contrast to the tranquillity of the Speyside Way are the scenes of activity at Boat of Garten and Dufftown stations where the railway has arisen Phoenix-like from the scene of dereliction left when train services were withdrawn.

While all trace of the Great North's presence may have vanished at Boat of Garten, the railway itself is very much alive. The Strathspey Railway Company was established in 1971 with a view to eventually re-opening the line from Aviemore as far as Grantown. In 1978 steam trains began running again to Boat of Garten and later the rails reached Broomhill, 9¼ miles from Aviemore, so once more passengers may enjoy the sight, sound (and smell!) that for so long characterised the country's railways. At both Aviemore and Boat of Garten stations there is a good deal to see - locomotives, rolling stock and a museum containing many fascinating artefacts while Broomhill later achieved fame as "Glenbogle" in the BBC's "Monarch of the Glen". More is in prospect as plans are already afoot to extend the railway to Grantown, along the old Highland Railway, a further 3½ miles.

Dufftown may not have figured largely in this book but legally it was the northern terminus of the Strathspey Railway. Here members of the Keith & Dufftown Railway Association have been hard at work restoring the ten mile link between the two towns and trains started running again in 2000. Unlike the Speyside Railway, which is largely steam worked, the trains are formed of old style diesel units giving an excellent view of the scenery along the route. At Dufftown itself there is a interesting collection of rolling stock, including one of the unusual "electro-diesel" locomotives and two ex-Brighton Belle Pullman cars, as well as a museum covering the history of the line.

Craigellachie

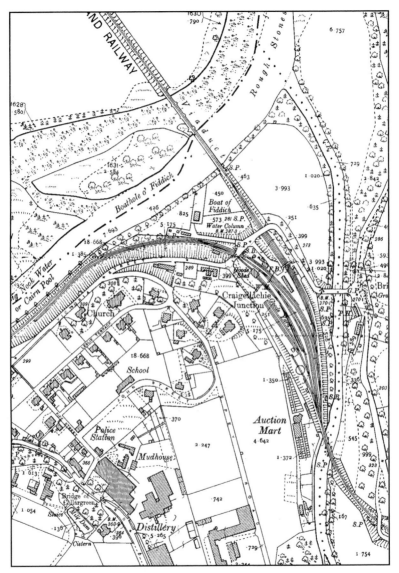

The station is closely confined by the rivers Fiddich and Spey. The main line from Aberdeen to Elgin is on the right with the Speyside line curving away to the left.

0 *yards*   100   200   300

Aberlour

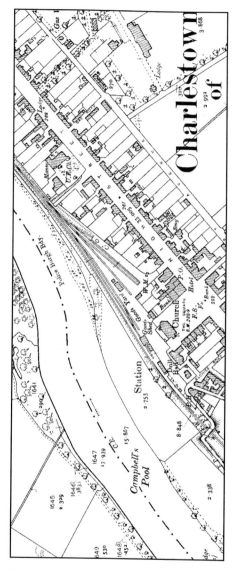

These maps of the stations on the Speyside line are taken from the Ordnance Survey 25" to 1 mile maps, 2nd edition (1902 - 1909).

They have been reduced by 50% for reproduction here.

All maps lead south (towards Boat of Garten) at the foot of the page.

The broken line which runs along the River Spey on some of the maps marks the county border between Morayshire (left) and Banffshire (right).

Abbreviations :

C	Crane
FB	Footbridge
FP	Footpath
GP	Guide Post
MP	Mile Post
MS	Mile Stone
P	Pump
PH	Public House
PO	Post Office
SB	Signal Box
SP	Signal Post
WM	Weighing Machine

The passing loop was not added until 1910, several years after this map was surveyed.

0 *yards*   100   200   300

Carron

Knockando

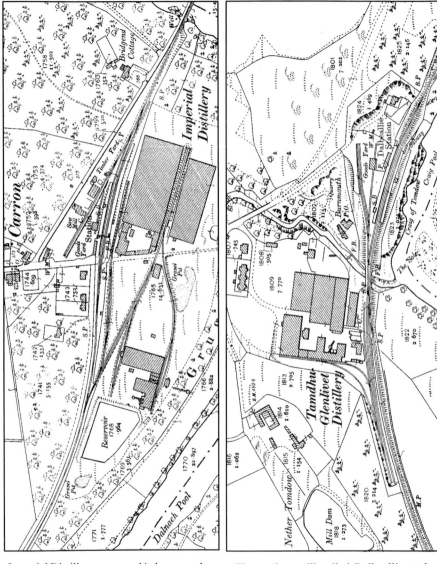

Imperial Distillery, squeezed in between the railway and river, dominates this small community. The owner of the sawmill chose a handy site alongside both road and railway.

The station, still called Dalbeallie at the time of the survey, is tucked into a steep hillside above the river. The subway, as opposed to a footbridge, is clearly marked.

Blacksboat

Ballindalloch

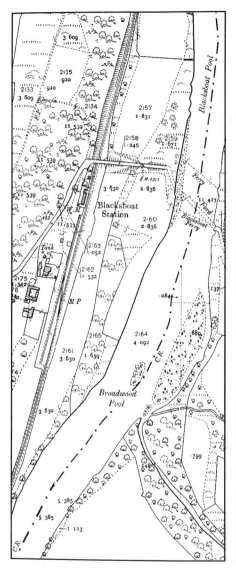

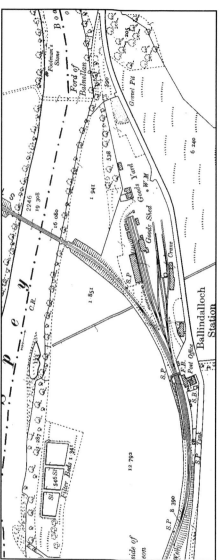

The ferry was still working when the survey was made. An extra siding was added on the west (left) side when the bridge was opened in 1911.

The size of the goods yard, compared with other stations, shows this was a busy place. The filter beds are for yet another distillery, Cragganmore, just off the map.

0 yards   100   200   300

Advie

Cromdale

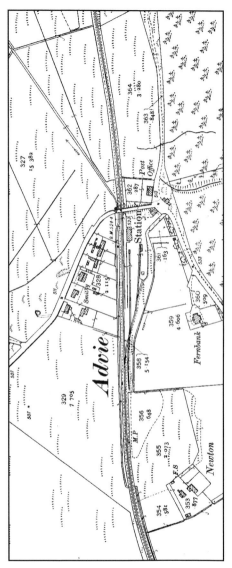

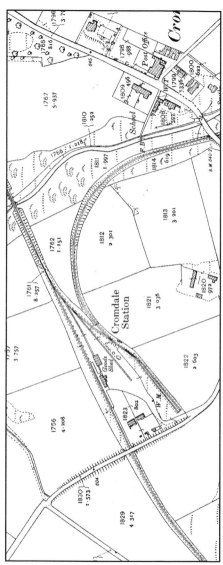

A small wayside station. Part of the trackbed is now used as the road to the local cemetery.

The line to Balmenach Distillery curves away to the right.

0 *yards*   100   200   300

Grantown   Nethybridge

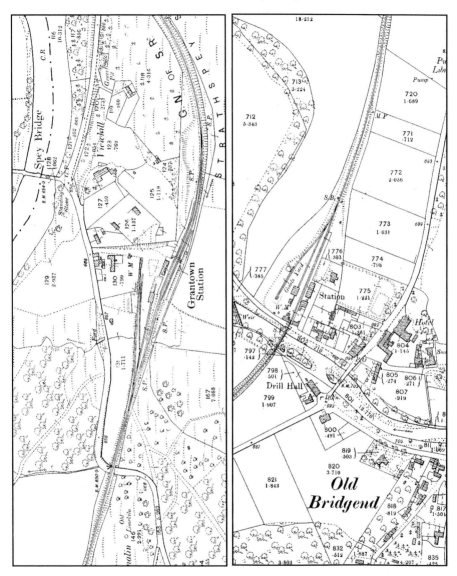

The proximity of the Spey Bridge led to the station being referred to as Grantown Bridge when the line was inspected prior to opening.

This was the orignal end of the line, hence the amount of vacant space alongside the goods yard, which was occupied by the usual terminal facilities, including turntable and locomotive shed.

Boat of Garten

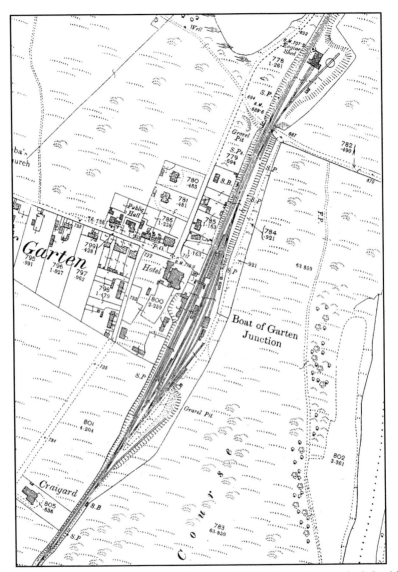

The double track at the top of the map shows the Highland main line on the left with the Great North to the right of it. The extensive layout allowed for exchange of traffic between the two companies.

0 yards   100   200   300

Appendix 1 : Opening and Closing Dates

Name	Dist	Opened	Closed Passenger	Goods
Craigellachie (a)	0	1.7.1863	6.5.1968	4.11.1968
Aberlour	2¾	1.7.1863	18.10.1965	15.11.1971
Dailuaine Halt	4¾	18.11.1933	18.10.1965	—
Dailuaine Distillery (b)	5	1905	—	4.11.1968
Carron	5½	1.7.1863	18.10.1965	4.11.1968
Imperial Distillery (c)	5¾	1897	—	4.11.1968
Imperial Cottages Halt	6	15.6.1959	18.10.1965	—
Knockando House (d)	7	1869	18.10.1965	—
Knockando Distillery (c)	7¾	16.10.1905	—	4.11.1968
Gilbey's Cottages Halt	8	15.6.1959	18.10.1965	
Knockando (e)	8¼	1.7.1899	18.10.1965	4.11.1968
Blacksboat	10½	1.7.1863	18.10.1965	2.11.1959
Ballindalloch	12¼	1.7.1863	18.10.1965	4.11.1968
Advie (1st location)	14½	1.7.1863	1.9.1868	1.9.1868
Advie (2nd location)	15¼	1.9.1868	18.10.1965	2.11.1959
Dalvey	17¼	1.7.1863	1.9.1868	1.9.1868
Dalvey Farm Halt	17½	15.6.1959	18.10.1965	—
Cromdale	21¼	1.7.1863	18.10.1965	4.11.1968
Grantown–on-Spey (f)	24¼	1.7.1863	18.10.1965	4.11.1968
Ballifurth Farm Halt	26¾	15.6.1959	18.10.1965	—
Nethybridge (g)	28¾	1.7.1863	18.10.1965	25.1.1965
Boat of Garten (h)	33½	1.8.1866	18.10.1965	2.11.1965

Notes

(a) Called Strathspey Junction until 1.6.1864.

(b) Exchange sidings for Dailuaine Distillery.

(c) Private siding.

(d) Private station for passengers only. Called Knockando unitil 2.10.1905.

(e) Opened as Tamdhu Siding 29.5.1896. Renamed Dalbeallie and opened for all traffic 1.7.1899. Renamed Knockando 2.10.1905. Private sidings for Tamdhu Distillery were off station yard.

(f) Grantown until 1.6.1912. Renamed Grantown-on-Spey (East) by BR.

(g) Called Abernethy until December 1867.

(h) Highland Railway station, opened 3.8.1863. Dates shown are for GNSR traffic.

Timber Sidings

A siding was authorised at Pollowick, about 1½ miles north of Cromdale, in August 1867, for timber from Lord Seafield's estate. Closure date unknown.

Four sidings were laid in to handle the large amount of timber felled on Speyside during and shortly after the Great War. These were :

(i) Knockando, 850 yards on the Carron side of Knockando station. Authorised 1917, closure date unknown.

(ii) Ballindalloch. $^3/_8$ mile north of Ballindalloch station. Opened January 1920. Closed June 1930.

(iii) Nethy Bridge, 250 yards north of Nethy Bridge station. opened July 1917. Closed April 1920.

(iv) Abernethy, ¾ mile beyond Nethy Bridge station. Opened July 1918. Closed September 1923.

Appendix 2 : Traffic

Source : GNSR and LNER papers.

Year ended 31st July 1865   Strathspey Railway

	Number	Income
Passengers - 1st class	11,103	£456
- 3rd and Excursion	22,962	£701
- Parliamentary	63,579	£1,406
Total Passengers	**97,644**	
Carriages and Horses		£31
Mails		£200
Goods, Minerals and Livestock		£1,892
Tolls payable by Keith and Dufftown Rly for use of Balvenie Extension*		£1,129
Other		£24
Total		**£5839**
Working expenses		£6,674
Operating loss		**£835**

* The line between Dufftown and Craigellachie was legally part of the Strathspey Railway.

Year ended 31st July 1903   Great North of Scotland Railway

Passengers

Passengers Booked	Number	Income
Between station on Speyside	56,871	£1,898
To and from stations beyond Speyside	44,483	£2,396
Throughout between Craigellachie and Boat of Garten	440	£108
	101,794	£4,402
Season tickets	721	£150
Parcels		£801
Totals		**£5,353**

Goods, Minerals and Livestock

Consigned	Livestock (trucks)	Goods/Minerals (tons)	
Between stations on Speyside	139	2,040	£458
Beyond Craigellachie	576	54,729	£6,328
Beyond Boat of Garten	108	4,464	£659
Through between Craigellachie and Boat of Garten	29	4,729	£420
Totals	**852**	**65,962**	**£7,865**
Deduct cartage			£253
			£7,612
Total (mails not included)			**£12,965**

Operating expenses

Traffic Department	£2,808
Locomotive Department	£3,117
Permanent Way Department	£1,882
Other charges	£2,313
Total	**£10,120**
Operating surplus	**£2,845**

1938   **London & North Eastern Railway**

Passengers

Station	Tickets	Income
Aberlour	6,386	£730
Carron	3,616	£241
Knockando	3,852	£338
Blacksboat	1,503	£151
Ballindalloch	1,598	£252
Advie	1,094	£155
Cromdale	928	£118
Grantown	1,613	£425
Nethy Bridge	1,639	£299
Boat of Garten	1,042	£189
Totals	**23,271**	**£2,898**

Merchandise/Minerals, Coal and Livestock

Stations	Merchandise & Minerals (tons)		Coal (tons)	Livestock (trucks)	
	In	Out	In	In	Out
Aberlour	3,431	3,477	4,344	92	11
Carron	5,352	2,935	3,316	7	5
Knockando	3,452	1,595	2,304	45	26
Ballindalloch & Blacksboat	5,231	4,781	5,287	78	189
Advie	483	46	127	32	51
Cromdale	2,972	1,262	1,806	29	39
Grantown	1,083	919	1,999	18	61
Nethy Bridge	1,065	77	756	9	13
Boat of Garten	815	10	26	3	11
Totals	**23,884**	**15,102**	**19,965**	**313**	**406**

58

Appendix 3 : Financial Performance of the Strathspey line

Source : GNSR papers.

Year ended 31st July 1869

Station expenses	£885
Maintenance	£965
Locomotives and guards	£845
10% on plant for interest and repairs	£500
Feu duties, rates and taxes	£450
Total (a)	**£3645**
Gross Revenue from branch	£4,420
Gross Revenue drawn on main line (a)	£1,610
Total Gross Revenue	**£6,030**
Net Revenue	**£2,385**
Interest on unproductive capital invested by GNSR in branch @ 5%	£12,510
Less Net Revenue	£2,385
Loss on branch	£10,125
Capital cost of railway	£250,000
Average return on capital	0.95%

No allowance made for Head Office charges.

(a) Derived from traffic exchanged with branch less 30% for working expenses.

Year Ended 31st July 1903

Gross Revenue	£12,965
Traffic expenses	£2,808
Locomotive department	£3,117
Permanent way costs	£1,882
Feu duties, taxes, etc	£1,162
Other charges, including Head Office	£1,150
Total	**£10,119**
Net Revenue	**£2,846**
Capital cost : Railway	£300,000
Plant (a)	£14,291
Total	**£314,291**
Average percentage interest on capital (b)	0.91%

(a) Assumed that 2½ locomotives, 10 carriages and 50 wagons were required to work the line.

(b) At this time the average return on the Company's shares was about 2.1%.

Bibliography

Great North of Scotland Railway Minute Books and Papers

Speyside Railway Minute Books and Papers

Highland Railway Minute Books

Morayshire Railway Minute Books

Inverness & Aberdeen Junction Railway Minute Books

LNER papers

Board of Trade Inspection Reports

Great North Review (various issues)

The Great North of Scotland Railway - A Guide   W Ferguson of Kinmundy.
David Douglas (1881)

The Great North of Scotland Railway (2nd Edition)   H A Vallance
David St.John Thomas (1989)

Regional History of the Railways of Great Britain, Vol.15   J Thomas & D Turnock
David St.John Thomas (1989)

Speyside Railways   Rosemary Burgess & Robert Kinghorn
Aberdeen University Press (1988)

Industrial Locomotives of Scotland

Industrial Railway Society (1976)

The Aviemore Line : Railway Politics in the Highlands 1882-98   N T Sinclair
Transport History Vol32 No.3 (November 1969)

Elgin Courant

***Blacksboat in May 1989 looking towards Boat of Garten. This was an isolated station
and remains one of the least altered, complete with one of the last GNSR goods sheds to
survive.*** *(Keith Fenwick)*

Acknowledgements

Editorial : Dick Jackson gratefully acknowledges the help given to him by a number of people, in particular George Boardman, Sandy Edward, Andrew Simpson, Neil Sinclair, Martin Smith, fellow members of the GNSRA and the staff of the National Archives of Scotland.

Layout and typesetting by Keith Fenwick

Printed by W Peters & Sons Ltd., Turriff.

All photographs are drawn from the Association's archives except where shown.

25" OS maps reproduced with kind permission of the Trustees of the National Library of Scotland.

This book first published 1996. Reprinted 2006 with additional material.

© 2006 Dick Jackson

Published by the Great North of Scotland Railway Association.
ISBN10 : 0 90234 317 3
ISBN13 : 978 0 90234 317 7

The Great North of Scotland Railway Association

The Association caters for all those interested in the history of the Great North of Scotland Railway and its constituent companies, as well as the LNER, British Railways and ScotRail periods. The Association promotes the study and collection of information, documents and illustrations relating to all aspects of the North East's railways. It also facilitates and co-ordinates members' research and provides information for modellers.

Members receive a quarterly journal containing articles, photographs, drawings and news of the railway, both historical and current. The Association produces a comprehensive series of Abstracts covering aspects of the railway in great detail. Members receive a discount on the range of books produced by the Association. Meetings and excursions are regularly organised for the benefit of members.

For further information, please contact the Membership Secretary, Craighall Cottage, Guildtown, Perth, PH2 6DF or visit the Association's website www.gnsra.org.uk.